FEDERAL HIGH COURT
VS
STATE HIGH COURT
Investigating the Jurisdictional Boundaries through the Cases

FEDERAL HIGH COURT
VS
STATE HIGH COURT
Investigating the Jurisdictional Boundaries through the Cases

EWERE ODIASE ESQ, ACIArb.
Legal Practitioner and Principal Partner,
ODIASE-LAWYERS CONSULTING

SPECTRUM BOOKS LIMITED
Ibadan
Abuja • Benin City • Jos • Lagos • Owerri • Zaria

www.spectrumbookslimited.com

Published by
Spectrum Books Limited
Spectrum House
Ring Road
P. M. B. 5612
Ibadan, Nigeria
e-mail: info@spectrumbookslimited.com

in association with
Safari Books (Export) Limited
1st Floor
17 Bond Street
St. Helier
Jersey JE2 3NP
Channel Islands, UK

First published, 2017

ISBN: 978-978-926-411-7

DEDICATION

This work is dedicated to the Almighty God, our help in ages past, and hope for years to come.

IN MEMORIAM

In loving memory of my dearly beloved father, Rev. E. V. Odiase (1937-2014), a Baptist preacher and consummate teacher, who introduced me to the splendour of written English, at an early age.

FOREWORD

The learned author of this treatise engaged in a thorough research and analysis of cases and authorities with the genuine aim of resolving once and for all or at least to a large extent, the much vexed and contentious issue of jurisdiction as relating to the Federal and State High Courts.

Much as the appellate and apex Courts of this country have, through numerous decisions, made pronouncements on the extent and limits of the jurisdiction of the Federal High Court, the legal battle on the issue unfortunately continues to rage either through inadvertence or deliberate effort of some lawyers to generate water from an igneous rock.

A recent example was when a counsel argued vigorously yet naively before us, that the Federal High Court has the sole jurisdiction to try any criminal matter whatsoever, provided it is filed by the office of the Attorney General of the Federation by virtue of Section 174 (1)of the 1999 Constitution and Section 7(4) of the Federal High Court Act and this includes all offences in the Criminal Code Act and the Penal Code being offences which the Attorney General of the Federation could initiate proceedings. This argument, no doubt, is against Section 251(3) of the 1999 Constitution which limits the criminal jurisdiction of the Federal High Court to matters in respect of which jurisdiction is conferred by Section 251(1).

This book will, indeed, bring salvation and redemption to the confused, the uninformed and the intransigent on the jurisdictional scope of our High Courts.

It is divided into three parts. The first part is a synopsis of the current state of the law on jurisdiction of our courts and of great value therein is the manner it clearly distinguished and dealt with borderline cases or grey areas on the issues of jurisdiction between the Federal High Court and the State High Court.

The second part is equally valuable, as it contains numerous cases and materials revealing the stance of the appellate courts on the issue of the limited jurisdiction of the Federal High Court.

The third part expectedly, is an admixture of cases and decisions reflecting the various views of the justices of the appellate courts.

To my mind, this book is quite timely, valuable, educative and informative. It is a veritable tool for lawyers, the bench and the academia for the proper understanding of the scope and limit of jurisdiction of the Federal and State High Courts.

I highly commend the author for his industry.

HON. JUSTICE S.C. OSEJI
Justice of the Court of Appeal,
Lagos Division

PREFACE

Federal High Court vs State High Court is a determined inquest into the boundaries, scope and contours of the exclusive jurisdiction of the Federal High Court vested by section 251 of the 1999 Constitution of the Federal Republic of Nigeria. The battle for the appropriate venue for ventilating the cases of litigants, especially when such pertain to matters involving the Federal Government or any of its agencies, became more intensely combative after the enactment of Decree No. 107 of 1993. The amendment of section 230 of the 1979 Constitution by the said decree metamorphosed into section 251 of the 1999 Constitution, following the repeal of Decree No. 107 of 1993 by Decree No. 63 of 1999.

The appellate courts have substantially streamlined the extent, scope and limit of the exclusive jurisdiction of the Federal High Court under section 251 of the constitution, as against the general jurisdiction of the State High Court, under section 272(1) of the same constitution.

Federal High Court vs State High Court is an effort to systematically survey the relevant decisions with a view to helping practitioners make a swift and informed choice of venue, particularly where the facts are not so straight forward.

ACKNOWLEDGEMENTS

It has been rewarding to contend with opposing counsel on the intricacies of section 251(1) of the 1999 Constitution dealing with the exclusive jurisdiction of the Federal High Court. The court-room debates have given rise to a robust rumination over the subject on my part.

This determined survey of legal authorities on the often vexed and hotly contested provision, is a tribute to the numerous counsel on the other side, for the inspiration.

The revered silk, G.R.I. Egonu (SAN) was of immense value and I appreciatehismagnanimity andencouragementinthecourse of this work. I am grateful for the kind guardiance of D.D. Dodo (SAN) at the onset of my legal career. All staff and solicitors of Odiase Lawyers Consulting, past andpresentto whom I owe debt of gratitude for the accomplishment of this modest contribution to legal knowledge. I shall not fail to mention Raymond Azi Esq., ArinzeAniemeka Esq., Ebiton Ugboka Esq., ChiomaAsindi(Mrs.), Chinedu Orji Esq., Donald Chinoso Esq., Stanley Ofor Esq., Ibrahim Segun Esq., Concilia Okolie (Miss) Sec/Admin., Marian Uso (Mrs.) Sec/Admin., Eze Victory (Miss.) Sec/Admin., Patrick Amuta Leg. Assist. and Collins Onah Leg. Assist.

I salute all whose direct and quiet inputs deserve mention but whose names were omitted due to space constraints. They are hereby deemed mentioned.

EWERE ODIASE ESQ. ACIArb.
Principal Partner
Odiase-Lawyers Consulting
odiaselawyers@yahoo.com, www.odiaselawyers.com

CONTENTS

TABLE OF CASES

Title

Abbas vs C.O.P (1998) 12 NWLR (Pt. 577) 308

Abiola & Sons Bottling Company Nigeria Limited & Anor vs First City Merchant Bank Limited (2013) LPELR-20387(SC), (2013) 4 MJSC. 122

Abidoye vs the Federal Republic of Nigeria (2014) 5 NWLR (Pt. 1399) 30

Adekoye and Ors vs Nigerian Security Printing Minting Company Ltd (2009) 5 NWLR (Pt. 1134) 322

Adelekan vs Ecu-Line NV (2006) 12 NWLR (Pt. 993) 33

Adesina vs Kola (1993) 6 NWLR (Pt. 298) 182 at 185

Adetayo vs Ademola (2010) 5 NWLR (Pt. 1215) p. 169

Adetona and 2 Ors vs Igele General Enterprises Ltd (2011) 7 NWLR (Pt. 1247) 535

Adisa vs Oyinwola (2000) 10 NWLR Pt. 674 at 116

A.G. of Lagos State vs A. G.of the Federation and 35 Ors (2014) 9 NWLR (Pt. 1412) 217

Akegbejo vs Ataga (1998) 1 NWLR (534) 459,

Ali vs. CBN (1997) 4 NWLR (Pt. 498) 192

Aliyu vs Federal Republic of Nigeria (2014) 5 NWLR (Pt. 1399) p. 101

Anazodo vs Pazmeck Inter Trade, Nigeria & Anor(2008) 6 NWLR (Pt. 1084) 529

A.P.G.A vs Anyanwu (2014) 7 NWLR (Pt. 1407) 541

Ayman Enterprises Limited vs Akuma Industries Limited & Ors (2003) 13 NWLR (Pt. 836) 22

Corporation (liquidator of United Commercial Bank Limited) :(1999) 2 NWLR (Pt. 591) 333

FGN vs Shobu (2014) 4 NWLR (Pt. 1396) 45

F.M.B.N. vs NDIC (1999) 2 NWLR (Pt. 591) 333

Gafar vs Government of Kwara State (2007) 4 NWLR (Pt. 1024) 375

Garba vs FCSC (1988) 1 NWLR (Pt. 71) 449

Gbagi vs Okpoko (2014) 4 NWLR (Pt. 1396) 136

George vs Federal Republic of Nigeria (2014) 5 NWLR (Pt. 1399) 1

Gulf Oil Nig Ltd vs F.B.I.R (1997) 7 N.W.L.R Part 514

Hallmark Bank Plc vs Obasanjo (2014) 4 NWLR (1397) 209,

Ikenne Local Government vs West African Portland Cement Plc (2012) All FWLR (Pt. 642) 1747

Integrated Timber and Plywood Products Ltd vs Union Bank Nigeria Plc (2006) 12 NWLR (Pt. 995) 483

Jammal Steel Structures Ltd vs African Continental Bank Ltd (1973) 1 All NLR (Pt. II) 208

Kalu vs FRN (2014) 1 NWLR (Pt. 1389) 479

KLM Royal Dutch Airlines vs Taher (2014) 3 NWLR (Pt. 1393) 137

Lagos State Internal Revenue Board vs Motorola Nigeria Limited (2012) LPELR-14712(CA)

Lawan vs Zenon Petroleum & Gas Ltd & ORS(2014) LPELR-23206(CA)

Madukolu vs Nkemdilim (1962) I All NLR 587

Maideribe vs Federal Republic Nigeria (2014) 5 NWLR (Pt. 1399) 68

Ministry of Works vs Tomas Nig. Ltd (2002) 2 NWLR (Pt. 752) 744

Mobil Producing Nigeria Unlimited vs Suffolk Petroleum Services Limited (2013) LPELR-21193 (CA)
National Bank vs Soyoye (1977) 5 SC 181
NDIC vs CBN (2002) 7 NWLR (Pt. 766) 272
NDIC vs FMBN (1997) 2 NWLR (Pt. 490) 735
NDIC vs Okem Enterprises Ltd (2004) 10 NWLR (Pt. 880) 107
NIDB vs Fembo (Nig.) Ltd (1997) 2 NWLR (Pt. 489) 543
Nigerian Aviation Handling Company limited vs Yinka World Investment limited & Anor 3 ilaw /ca/l/916/2007
Nkuma vs Joseph Otunuya Odili & Ors (2006) 6 NWLR (Pt. 977)
NNPC vs Okwor (1998) 7 NWLR (Pt. 559) 637
Nwafia vs Ububa(1966) NMLR p. 219
Oamen vs. Owenan (1993) 8 NWLR (311) 358,
Obiuwebi vs CBN (35) (2011) 7 NWLR (Pt. 1247) 465
Ochala vs Federal Republic of Nigeria (2013) LPELR-21386(CA)
Odutola vs. University of Ilorin (2004) 12 SCN 236
Ogbuanyinya vs Okudo (1979) 6–9 SC. 32
Okewu vs FRN (2012) 9 NWLR (Pt. 1305) 327,
Okorocha vs PDP (2014) 7 NWLR (Pt. 1406) 213
Okoye vs. Nigerian Construction & Furniture Co. (1991) 6 NWLR (Pt. 199) P401
Oladipo vs NCSB (2009) 12 NWLR (Pt. 1156) 563
Oloha vs Akereja (1988) 7SC (Pt. 11) at 11–12
Olubeko vs Federal Republic of Nigeria (2014) LPELR-22632 (CA)
Olutola vs Unilorin (2004) NWLR (Pt. 905) 416
Omosowan & 2 Ors vs Chiedozie (1998) 9 NWLR (Pt. 566) 477
Onuorah vs Kaduna Refining and Petrochemical Company Ltd, (2005) 6 NWLR (Pt. 921) 393

Onwudiwe vs F.R.N. (2006) 10 NWLR (Part 988) 382
Opia vs INEC (2014) 7NWLR (Pt. 1407) 431
Orhiunu vs Federal Republic of Nigeria (2005) 1 NWLR (Pt. 906)39
Petrojessica Enterprises Ltd vs Leventis Technical Co. Ltd (1992) 5 NWLR (Part 244) 675
PDP vs INEC (1999) 11 NWLR (Pt. 626) 200
PDP vs T. Sylva & 2 Ors (2012) All FWLR (Pt. 1316) 85
Penok Ltd vs Hotel Presidential Ltd (1982) 12 SC 1
Ports and Cargo Handlings Service Company Limited & Ors vs Migfo Nigeria Limited & Anor(2012) 18 NWLR (Pt. 1333) 555
Progressive Insurance Co. Ltd vs Adepoju (1991) 1 NWLR (Pt. 166) 248
Rabe vs Federal Republic of Nigeria (2013) LPELR-20163(CA)
S.E.C vs Kasumu (2001) 10 NWLR (Part 1150) 509
Shell Dev. Co (Nig.) Ltd vs FBIR (1996) 8 NWLR (Part 466) 256
Shell Pet. Dev. Co. (Nig.) Ltd vs Isaiah (2001) 11 NWLR (Pt. 723) 168
Shittu vs Nigerian Agricultural & Cooperative Bank Limited & Ors (2001) 10 NWLR (Pt. 721) 298
SLB Consortium Ltd vs NNPC (2011) 9 NWLR (Pt. 1252) 317
Society BIC S.A. vs Charzin Ind. Limited (2014) 4 NWLR (Pt. 1398) 499
Stanley Ossai vs The Federal Republic of Nigeria (2012) LPELR-19669 (CA)
Sudan Airways Company Limited vs Surajo Mohammed Abdullahi
(1998) 1 NWLR (Part 532)156
Tanarewa (Nigeria) Limited vs Arzai (2005) 5 NWLR (Pt. 919) 593,

The Shell Petroleum Development Company of Nigeria Limited vs Chief G.B.A. Tiebo & Ors (2005) 9 NWLR (Pt. 931) 439

The Shell Petroleum Development Company of Nigeria Limited vs Otelemaba Maxon and Ors (2001) 9 NWLR (Pt. 719) 541

Trade Bank Plc vs Benilux (Nig.) Ltd (2003) 9 NWLR (Part 825) 416

Tukur vs GongolaState (1989) 4 NWLR (Pt. 117) 517

Udo vs Orthopedic Hospital Management Board (1993) 7 NWLR (Pt. 304) 139

Unity line Plc vs Usman (2014) 6 NWLR (Pt. 1404) 546

United Parcel Service vs Kosoko Adeyosoye (2010) LPELR-CA/B/167/2005

University of Abuja vs Ologe (1996) 4 NWLR (Pt. 445) 706

University of Ilorin Teaching Hospital vs Akilo (2001) 4 NWLR (Pt. 703) 246;

Uwaifo vs Attorney General, Bendel State (1983) NCLR 1 and Adesina vs Kola (1993) 6 NWLR (Pt. 298) 182

Yar'adua vs Yandoma(2015) 4 NWLR (Pt. 1448) p. 123 at 160 para G-H

7-up Bottling Co. Ltd vs Abiola & Sons Bottling Co. Ltd (1996) 7 NWLR (Pt. 463) 714

TABLE OF STATUTES

Admiralty Jurisdiction Act Cap 5 Laws of the Federation, 2004
Section l (1) of the Constitution of the Federal Republic of Nigeria, 1979
Section 42(2)
Section 230
Section 230(1)(f)
Section 277
Section 277(1)
Constitution of the Federal Republic of Nigeria, 1999
Concurrent Legislative List
Exclusive Legislative List
Section 4(2)
Section 36
Section 174(1)
Section 232(1)
Section 251(1)
Section 251(1)(a)
Section 251(1)(b)
Section 251(1)(c)
Section 251(1)(d)
Section 251(1)(e)
Section 251(1)(f)
Section 251(1)(g)
Section 251(1)(h)
Section 251(1)(i)
Section 251(1)(j)

Section 251(1)(k)
Section 251(1)(l)
Section 251(1)(m)
Section 251(1)(n)
Section 251(1)(o)
Section 251(1)(p)
Section 251(1)(q)
Section 251(1)(r)
Section 251(1)(s)
Section 251(1)(p)(q)(r)
Section 252 (2)
Section 251(3)
Section 272(1)
Section 272(1)–(3)
S. 318 (1)
Constitution (Suspension and Modification) Decree No. 107 of 1993
Section 230(1)(a)
Section 230(1)(d
Section 230(1)(f)
Companies and Allied Matters Act Cap 20 Laws of the Federation of Nigeria 2004... *Section 387 of the Act....*
Section 393 of the Act... s
Section 396 of the Act ...
Sections 393, 996, 398 and 399
Central Bank of Nigeria Act, Cap 47 Laws of the Federation of Nigeria 1990
Section 39 of the
Corrupt Practices and Other related Offences Act 2000
Section 22(3) of the
Criminal Code Cap 32 Vol. 2 Laws of Lagos State of Nigeria

1994
Section 517 of the
Section 203 of the criminal code
Section 104 of the
Criminal Code Cap 32 Vol. 2, Laws of Lagos State of Nigeria 1994
Decree No 17 of 1984
Section 3 (3)
Decree No. 59 of 1991
Section 1(1) (h)
Decree 60 of 1991
Section 7(6) (b)
Decree No. 18 of 1994
Decree No. 62 of 1999
Decree No. 63 of 1999
Electoral Act, 2010
Section 68 (1) (C) of the
Failed Banks (Recovery of Debts) and Financial Malpractices in Banks Decree No. 18 of 1994
Federal High Court Act
Federal High Court (Civil Procedure) rules
Federal High Court Act, No. 23 of 1973
Section 1(1) of the Act,
Federal High Court Act, 1973 (Cap 134 Laws of the Federation of Nigeria, 1990)
Federal High Court Act Cap 134 Laws of the Federation of Nigeria, 1990
Section7(i)(b)(ii) and 8(i) S. 7(1)(c)(ii)
Section7(6)
Federal Mortgage Bank Decree No. 82 of 1993
sections 5(1)(a) and 6(1)(a) & (b)

Federal Revenue Court Act, Cap 134

Indian Hemp Act, volume 7, Cap 16, Laws of the Federation of Nigeria, 2004

Money Laundering Prohibition Act, 2004

Section 19(1)

Nigerian ports Authority Act Chapter N.126 Laws of the Federation of Nigeria 2004

National Drug Law Enforcement Agency Act, Cap N30 Laws of the Federation of Nigeria, 2004

Section 11(c)

Section 26(1)

Oyo State Internal Revenue Board Amended Edict, 1997

Section 28

Pensions Act, Cap 346 Laws of the Federation

Personal Income Tax Decree (PITD) No. 104 of 1993

Taxes and Levies (Approved List for Collection) Decree No. 21 1998

Section 1 & 2

Trademark Act, 1965,

Value Added Tax Act Cap VI Laws of the Federal Republic of Nigeria, 2004

Weights And Measure Act (Cap 467) Laws of the Federation of Nigeria, 1990

INTRODUCTION

This work is in three parts. *The first part* is a synopsis of the current state of the law, on the jurisdictional relationship between the Federal High Court and the State High Court, distilled from relevant judgments of the appellate courts. It deals with ***borderline cases*** wherein the character of a given case, in terms of the parties or subject matter tend to create an opening for challenging the competence of the forum/venue, that is to say, whether the case should properly be instituted in the State High Court or the Federal High Court, bearing in mind that the contest between proponents and opponents in jurisdictional conflicts can be stiff and robust.

The second part adopts a "cases and materials" approach in presenting the position of the appellate courts in disputes wherein the jurisdiction of the Federal High Court, were directly in issue.

The third part, A and B, comprise a cocktail of appellate decisions on the vexed question of the jurisdiction of the Federal High Court over cases affecting the Federal Government or any of its agencies as well as the interpretation of the provisions of section 251(3) of the said constitution which deals with criminal cases arising from the items listed under section 251(1) of the grundnorm.

PART 1

Chapter 1

Jurisdiction, Judicially Defined

1.1. Jurisdiction has been broadly defined as the limits imposed on the power of a validly constituted court to hear and determine issues between persons seeking to avail themselves of its process by reference to the subject matter of the issues or to the persons between whom the issues are founded or to the kind of relief sought, per **Muhammad, JSC** *Yar'adua v. Yandoma*[(1)]

> The term jurisdiction denotes a court's power to entertain and determine a case or action. Also termed *Coram judice* (competent jurisdiction), the term judicial jurisdiction, denotes the legal power and authority of a court to make a decision that binds the parties to any matter properly brought before it. See *Dosumu v. NNPC.*[(2)]

The jurisdiction to try a matter is key to the validity and potency of a judgment.

> A judgment given without jurisdiction creates no legal obligation and does not confer any right to any of the parties. See *Attorney General of Lagos State v. the*

1. (2015)4NWLR (Pt. 1448) Page 123 at 160, paragraph G
2. (2014) 6 NWLR (Pt. 1403) Page 282 at 305, paragraph D

Attorney General of the Federation and 35 Ors[3] per **Muhammad JSC.**

1.2. It was Bairamian F.J who famously held in *Madukolu v. Nkemdilim* [4] thus;

> Any defect in competence is fatal, for the proceedings are a nullity, however well conducted and decided.

Apparently, a defect in competence is extrinsic to the adjudication of the proceedings. Thus a court which lacks jurisdiction by any reason is bereft of competence to try the case in question.

1.3. Fixed Elements of Jurisdiction

The parameters for the determination of jurisdiction to try a case was adumbrated in *Madukolu v. Nkemdilim* (supra) per **Bairamian F.J** (as he then was) while considering the competence of an irregular proceeding commenced on the strength of an order for retrial issued *ultra vires,* by an appellate court.

1.4. The ingredients of jurisdiction are as follows:

a. The court or tribunal must be properly constituted with the number and qualification of its members.

b. The subject matter of the action must be within its jurisdiction, and there is no feature in the case

3. (2014) 9 NWLR (Pt. 1412) Page 217 at 249, Paragraph D
4. (1962) I All NLR 587

which prevents the court from exercising its jurisdiction.

c. The action is initiated by due process of law and any condition precedent to the exercise of its jurisdiction has been fulfilled.

1.5. The apex court has consistently validated the above pre-conditions. See *Ogbuanyinya v. Okudo* (5) On the 14th of February, 2014, the Supreme Court upheld the three main pre-conditions of competent proceedings in the celebrated case of *Society BIC S.A. v. Charzin Industries Limited* (6)

1.6. Exclusive Jurisdiction of the Federal High Court

The main sources of the jurisdiction of the Federal High Court are: the Constitution of the Federal Republic of Nigeria 1999, the Federal High Court Act, and the Federal High Court (Civil Procedure) rules for the time being in force, as well as any jurisdiction which may be conferred by any other Act of the National Assembly.

The provision of section 251 of the Constitution (supra), reproduced hereunder, constitute the principal yardstick for the consideration of the jurisdiction of the Federal High Court.

> 251(1) Not withstanding anything to the contrary contained in this constitution and in addition to such other jurisdiction as may be conferred upon it by an Act of the National Assembly, the Federal High Court

5. (1979) 6 – 9 SC. 32
6. (2014) 4 NWLR (Pt. 1398) Page 499 at 534, Para. E–G

shall have and exercise jurisdiction to the exclusion of any other court in civil cases and matters.

Federal Revenue

a. relating to the revenue of the Government of the Federation in which the said Government or any organ thereof or a person suing or being sued on behalf of the said Government is a party;

Federal Taxation

b. connected with or pertaining to the taxation of companies and other bodies established or carrying on businesses in Nigeria and all other persons subject to federal taxation;

Customs and Excise

c. connected with or pertaining to customs and excise duties, including any claim by or against the Nigerian Customs Service or any member or officer thereof, arising from the performance of any duty imposed under any regulation relating to customs and excise duties and export duties;

Banking

d. connected with or pertaining to banking, banks, other financial institutions, including any action between one bank and another, any action by or against the Central Bank of Nigeria arising from banking, foreign exchange, coinage legal tender, bills of exchange, letters of credit, promissory notes and other fiscal measures provided that this paragraph shall not apply to any dispute between an individual customer and his bank in respect of transactions between the individual customer and the bank;

Operation of CAMA

e. arising from the operation of the Companies and Allied Matters Act (CAMA) or any other enactment replacing the operations of companies incorporated under the Companies and Allied Matters Act;

Copyrights, Trademarks, etc.

f. any Federal enactment relating to copyright, patency, designs, trademarks and passing off, Industrial monopolies, combines and trusts, standard of goods and commodities and industrial standards;

Admiralty and Shipping

g. any admiralty jurisdiction, including shipping and navigation on the River Niger or River Benue and their affluents and on such other inland waterways as may be designated by any enactment to be an international waterway, all federal ports (including the constitution and powers of the port authorities, for federal ports) and carriage by sea;

Diplomatic Matters

h. diplomatic, consular and trade representation;

Citizenship and Visas

i. citizenship, naturalisation and aliens, deportation of persons who are not citizens of Nigeria, extradition, immigration into and emigration from Nigeria, passport and visas;

Bankruptcy

j. Bankruptcy and insolvency;

Carriage by Air

k. aviation and safety of aircraft;

Firearms

l. arms, ammunition and explosives;

Drugs

m. drugs and poisons;

Mining

n. mines and minerals (including oil fields, oil mining, geological survey and natural gas);

Weights

o. weights and measures;

Actions against the Federal Government and Its Agencies

p. the administration or the management and control of the Federal Government or any of its agencies;

q. subject to the provisions of this constitution, the operation and interpretation of this constitution in so far as it affects the Federal Government or any of its agencies;

r. any action or proceeding for a declaration or injunction affecting the validity of any executive or administrative action or decision by the Federal Government or any of its agencies; and

s. such other jurisdiction, civil or criminal and whether to the exclusion of any other court or not, as may be conferred upon it by an Act of the National Assembly;
Provided that nothing in the provisions of paragraphs (p), (q) and (r) of this subsection shall prevent a person from seeking redress against the Federal Government or any of its agencies in an action for damages, injunction or specific performance where the action is based on any enactment, law or equity.

Treason and Criminal Offences Related to Jurisdiction Conferred by S.251(1)

(1) The Federal High Court shall have and exercise jurisdiction and powers in respect of treason, treasonable felony and allied offences.

(2) The Federal High Court shall also have and exercise jurisdiction and powers in respect of criminal cases and matters in respect of which jurisdiction is conferred by subsection 1 of this section.

Tenure Expiration and Vacancy of National Assembly Seat

(3) The Federal High Court shall have and exercise jurisdiction to determine any question as to whether the term of office or a seat of a member of the Senate or House of Representatives has ceased or his seat has become vacant.

1.7. "Not Withstanding", Judicially Defined

It is to be noted that section 251 of the constitution as reproduced above is commenced with the phrase *"not withstanding"* which has been judicially defined contextually in a number of cases. Uwaifo JSC in the case of *NDIC v. Okem Enterprises Limited* (7) held thus:

> when the term 'Not withstanding' is used in a section of a statute, it is meant to exclude an impinging or impeding effect of any other provision of the statute or other subordinate legislation , so that the said section may fulfill itself. It follows that as used in section 251(1) of the 1999 Constitution, no provision of that constitution shall be capable of undermining that section" p. 182, para. H

The Federal High Court as a Court of Enumerated Jurisdiction

1.8. The exclusive jurisdiction of the Federal High Court is not at large. It is circumscribed and limited principally, by the items and subjects listed in section 251 of the 1999 Constitution.

7. (2004) 10 NWLR (Pt. 880) 107

1.9. In the case of *Opia v. INEC* (8) the Supreme Court held thus:

> It must be noted that all the matters that fall within the exclusive jurisdiction of the Federal High Court, under section 251 of the 1999 Constitution (supra), have been specifically listed out. The legal implication is that the nature of the declaration being sought for it to be within the exclusive jurisdiction of the Federal High Court, must be in respect of the major items enumerated under the said section 251 (supra).
>
> The draftsman in no mistaken terms painstakingly itemised the subject matters within the exclusive jurisdiction of the Federal High Court," per **Galadima JSC**. See also *Olutola v. Unilorin.*(9)

1.10. The case of *Opia v. INEC* (supra) (10) is very instructive and decisive, in that it was clearly determined that the proper cannon of interpretation of section 251 of the constitution is *expressio unius est exclusio alterius*. This means that the express mention of one thing in a statutory provision, automatically excludes any other. See also, *PDP v. INEC* (11), *Buhari v. Dikko Yusuf* (12), *Udo v. Orthopaedic Hospital Management Board*(13), **Halsbury's Laws of England** (14).

8. (2014) 7NWLR (Pt. 1407) p. 431 at 459 – 460, Para. G – A
9. (2004) NWLR (Pt. 905) Page 416.
10. (2014) 7 NWLR (Pt. 1407) [page 431 at 464, Para. D – F].
11. (1999) 11 NWLR (Pt. 626) 200
12. (2003) 14 NWLR (Pt. 841) 446
13. (1993) 7 NWLR (Pt. 304) 139
14. 4th Edition, paragraph 876

1.11. The appellate court, while pronouncing on the technique employed by the draftsman and the proper approach for the construction of section 251 of the constitution, propounded a clear and unambiguous position of the law in the case of *Oladipo v. NCSB* [15] viz:

> The implication of this technique is that the said Federal High Court is actually a court of enumerated jurisdiction.

In explaining the meaning of the concept of *"enumerated jurisdiction"*, the court had this to say:

> That is a court whose jurisdiction is delineated in relation only to the subject matter enumerated therein. It would, therefore, amount to wreaking havoc on the express letters and intendment of the said section 251 to construe it as granting a **carte blanche** to deal with every conceivable matter that is beyond those expressly enumerated.
>
> The effect of the circumscription of the jurisdiction of the court to those eighteen major items is that whenever the question of jurisdiction of the court is canvassed, attention ought to be focused on the subject matter of the suit. If the subject matter of the suit cannot be pitch-forked into any of those eighteen major items, then that court is not the proper forum for the ventilation of the action". Quoted with approval by **Galadima JSC** in *Opia v. INEC* [16].

---

15. (2009) 12 NWLR (Pt. 1156) page 563 at 585 Para. C - F
16. (2014) 7 NWLR (Pt. 1407) [page 431 at 460 Para. B – E].

Other Sources of Jurisdiction of the Federal High Court

1.12. In addition to the subject matters listed under section 251, of the constitution, the Federal High Court also reserves exclusive jurisdiction over certain subject matters, pursuant to specific provisions in Acts of the National Assembly. In the case of *Kalu v. FRN*[17] **Eko JCA** held thus:

> Section 251 of the constitution is not exhaustive on the jurisdiction of the Federal High Court.
>
> Section 252 (2) of the same constitution expressly empowers the National Assembly to enact laws that may confer additional jurisdiction or power on the Federal High Court, notwithstanding the provisions of section 251(1) of the constitution, if it is 'necessary or desirable for enabling the court more effectively to exercise its jurisdiction'. Pursuant to this, the National Assembly has provided in section 19(1) of the Money Laundering Prohibition Act 2004 that: 'The Federal High Court shall have exclusive jurisdiction to try offences under this Act'. The constitutional authority for enacting this provision is not in doubt.

Jurisdiction of the State High Court over Subject Matters not Itemised under Section 251 of the 1999 Constitution

1.13. It is beyond doubt that the State High Court reserves general jurisdiction over matters *excluded* under section 251 (1) of the constitution (supra).

17. (2014) 1 NWLR (Pt. 1389) pg 479 at 545 Para. D-f

1.14. Notwithstanding the parties to the action, where the jurisdiction of the Federal High Court is canvassed as against the jurisdiction of the State High Court, the focus automatically shifts to the subject matter of the case.

1.15. An examination of the provisions of Section 272 (1) of the constitution (supra) will illuminate the clearly defined boundaries of both courts under the law.

1.16. "272 (1) subject to the provisions of section 251 and other provisions of this constitution, the High Court of a state shall have jurisdiction to hear and determine any civil proceedings in which the existence or extent of a legal right, power, duty, liability, privilege, interest, obligation or claim is an issue or to hear and determine any criminal proceedings, involving or relating to any penalty, forfeiture, punishment or other liability in respect of an offence committed by any person".

1.17. From the clear wordings of the above provision, the era of unlimited jurisdiction of the State High Court is gone. It ended with the 1979 Constitution which expressly stated that the State High Court shall have "unlimited jurisdiction". With the absence of that critical phrase, the tenor and extent of the original, as well as the supervisory jurisdiction of the State High Court is moderated, modified and qualified. In the case of *Society Bic S.A. v. Charzin Industries Limited,*(18) the Supreme Court

18. (2014) 4 NWLR (Pt. 1398) [page 495 at 540 Para. H

held thus:

> The jurisdiction of the State High Court is enormous but not unlimited, per **Rhodes-Vivour JSC**.

1.18. A more historical perspective of the current character of the jurisdiction of the State High Court is contained in the judgment of **Abba Aji JCA** in *Compagnie General De Geophysique Nig. Limited v. Anidi*[19] where it was held thus:

> In effect, S.7 (6) of the Federal High Court (Amended) Act, Decree No. 60 of 1991 and section 230(1) of the Constitution (suspension and modification) Decree No. 107 of 1993, jointly limited the unlimited jurisdiction of the State High Court and gave the Federal High Court exclusive jurisdiction in certain matters and these provisions were reinforced as section 251(1) of the 1999 Constitution.

1.19. Although there is no comprehensive list, encapsulating the jurisdiction of the State High Court, there is no doubt that its jurisdictional perimeter has been prescribed under section 272 (1)–(3) of the 1999 Constitution with reference to section 251 of the constitution.

1.20. In the case of *Gafar v. Government of Kwara State* [20] D-F, the Supreme Court held thus:

> Courts are creatures of statute and it is the statute that

19. (2005) LPELR PP31-33 Para. C-D.
20. (2007) 4 NWLR (Pt. 1024) Page 375 at 408 Para.

> created a particular court that will also confer on it, its jurisdiction"...The legislature and not the court may extend the jurisdiction and it is the function of the court in its duty of interpretation, to expound the jurisdiction of the court and certainly not to expand it, per **Ogbuagu JSC.**

Definition of the Phrase, "subject to"

1.21. Section 272 (1) of the constitution commences with the phrase, "subject to". This phrase has been defined judicially in the case of *Tukur v. Gongola State* (21). It was held thus:

> The expression "subject to", subordinates the provisions of the subject section to the section referred to, which is intended not to be affected by the latter. See *L.S.D.P.C v. Foreign Finance Corporation,* per **Obaseki JSC.**

1.22. In NDIC *(liquidators of Allied Bank Plc) v. Okem Enterprises Limited* (22) the Supreme Court held thus:

> It must therefore be understood that 'subject to' introduces a condition, a restriction, a limitation, a proviso. See *Oke v. Oke* (1974) 1 All NLR (Pt. 1) 443 at 450. It subordinates the provisions of the subject section to the section empowered by reference thereto and which is intended not to be diminished by the subject section. See *LSDPC v. Foreign Finance Corporation* (1987) 1 NWLR (Pt. 50)413 at 461, *Aqua*

21. (1989) 4NWLR (Pt. 117)P31-33 Para. C-D.
22. (2004) 10 NWLR (Pt. 880) 107

Limited v. Ondo State Sports Council (1988) 4 NWLR (Pt. 91) 622 at 655. The expression generally implies that what the section is subject to, shall govern, control and prevail over what follows in that subject section of the enactment", per **Uwaifo JSC.**

1.23. The effect of the phrase "subject to", section 251 (1), as used in section 272 (1) of the constitution, is that the judicial powers of the state shall be exercised by the State High Court, except with respect to items and subjects covered by section 251 of the same constitution.

Chapter 2

Borderline Cases

1.24. Lawyers are often confronted with cases which we categorise as borderline cases. They exhibit features which seem to bring them within the exclusive jurisdiction of the Federal High Court, only on a more careful examination, to lend greater weight to the State High Court as a choice of venue.

1.25. The first key to the resolution of these borderline cases is the principle of law that; "where part of the claim is within the jurisdiction of the court and the other is outside the jurisdiction, the court would decline jurisdiction, if a resolution of the case would involve inquiry or pronouncement on the aspect of the case which is not within the jurisdiction of the court". See *Nwafia v. Ububa*[23] per **Idigbe JSC**.

1.26. The second key to the resolution of any borderline case is the principle that the Federal High Court may only exercise jurisdiction where the jurisdiction over the subject matter as well as jurisdiction over the parties co-exist. Where any is absent, the Federal High Court will

23. (1966) NMLR Pg. 219 at 222

decline jurisdiction. In the case of *Enterprise Bank Plc v. Aroso* (24), the Supreme Court held thus:

> When the jurisdiction of the Federal High Court is in issue, the following must co-exist.
>
> (a) The parties or a party must be the Federal Government or its agency;
>
> (b) subject matter of the litigation.
>
> Satisfying the above is not the end of the matter. The pleadings of the plaintiff must be carefully examined so as to understand the facts and circumstances of the case in order to determine if the claims are within the jurisdiction of the court.
>
> It is clearly not enough only to have an agency of the Federal Government as a party before the Federal High Court has jurisdiction," per **Rhodes-Vivour JSC**.

Power of High Court to Transfer a Case he has no Juridiction to Determine

1.27. Section 22(3) of the Federal High Court Act states as follows: "Nothwithstanding anything to the contrary in any law, no cause or matter shall be struck out by the High Court of a State or of the Federal Capital Territory, Abuja on the ground that such cause or matter was taken in the High Court instead of the Court, and the Judge before whom such cause or matter is brought may cause such cause or matter to be transferred to the appropriate Judicial Division of the court in accordance with such rules of court as may be in force in that High Court or

24. (2014) 3 NWLR (Pt. 1394) Page 256 at 291 Para. E-G.

made under any enactment or law empowering the making of rules of court generally, which enactment or law shall by virtue of this subsection be deemed also to include power to make rules of court for the purpose of this subsection." The tenor and intendment of this subsection is that the State High Court can validly make an order of a transfer of a case from itself to a court of different juridiction. *A.D.H LTD V. A.T LTD*[(25)]

1.28. However, it is of note that where the rules or enabling law of a given State High Court does not make provision for the transfer of a case over which it lacks juridiction, such State High Court cannot transfer the suit to a court with appropriate juridction. The rules of each State High Court have the final say on the point.

In the case of Fasaking Foods (Nig.) Ltd. V. Martins Babatunde Shosanya,[(26)] OGBUAGU, J.S.C held thus:
"Under the said High Court of Lagos State (Civil Procedure) Rules, 1972, there is no rule of procedure, which enables that court, to transfer a cause or matter, to the Federal High Court. That court, cannot even in the circumstance, resort to or fall back to the practice and procedure in England as there appears to be no such provision for transfer from a High Court to the Federal High Court. So, as it stood or stands, the Lagos State House of Assembly, has not made any provision for the transfer of a cause or matter to the Federal High Court. See Aluminium etc. v. N.P.A. (infra). I am aware that while the Federal High Court can transfer a cause or matter to a State High Court, by virtue of section 22(2) of the (Federal High Court) Act, there is no such provision applicable at least, in the Lagos State High

25 (2006) LPERLR-583(SC) (Pp.13-14, Paras. G-E) Per Pat Acholonu, JSC.

26 (2006) LPELR-1244(SC)(P.14, Paras.C-G)

Court Rules. See Aluminium Manufacturing Co. (Nig.) Ltd. v N.P.A. (1987) 1 NSCC Vol. 18 Page 224 at 234; (1987) 1 NWLR (Pt.51) 475; (1987) 1 SCNJ 94.

Borderline Cases Involving Fundamental Human Rights Application

1.29. In the case of *Tukur v. The Government of Gongola State* [(27)], the Supreme Court held thus:

> If any consideration and determination of the civil rights and obligations, in matters outside the jurisdiction of the Federal High Court inextricably involves a consideration and determination of the breach or threatened breach of any of the fundamental rights provisions, the exercise of jurisdiction which the Federal High Court does not possess is a nullity. The lack of jurisdiction inexorably nullifies the proceedings and judgment. It is, therefore, an exercise in futility, per **Obaseki JSC**.

1.30. Dealing with the provision of the 1979 Constitution which vests jurisdiction in both the Federal High Court as well as the High Court of the state (by implications of the Fundamental Human Right Enforcement Rules) to try cases for the enforcement of Fundamental Human Rights, the Supreme court, in the same case of *Tukur v. The Government of Gongola State* (supra) held thus:

---

27 (1989) 4NWLR (Pt 117) Pg. 517 at 547 Para.

> Since the jurisdiction conferred by S. 42 (2) of the 1979 Constitution is a special jurisdiction and made subject to the provisions of the constitution, the enforcement of the fundamental rights in matters outside the jurisdiction of the Federal High Court is not within, and cannot be in the contemplation of the section, per **Obaseki JSC** at 547 Para. A-B.

1.31. In the above case, it was held that since the complain of breach of fundamental human rights was based on a chieftaincy matter, the Federal High Court could not entertain the case because it had no jurisdiction over a chieftaincy matter which was the foundation of the case.

1.32 In the similar case of *Gafar v. Government of Kwara State* (28). The Supreme Court held thus:

> The Law in this respect is also trite that where ancillary or incidental or accessory claim or claims are so inextricably tied to or bound up with the main claims before the court in a suit, a court cannot adjudicate over them, where it has no jurisdiction to entertain the main claims, if such incidental or ancillary claims cannot be determined without a determination at the same time of the main claims, or where the determination of such incidental or ancillary claims must necessarily involve a consideration or determination of the main claims. See *Tukur v.*

28 (2007) 4 NWLR (Pt. 1024) P. 375 SC at 3967 Para. B-F

Government of Gongola State (1989) 4 NWLR (Pt. 117) 517 at 546–54. In the instant case, it is not possible to determine the appellant's claim that his fundamental rights have been breached by the respondents without necessarily wading into the indictment of the appellant in the report of the commission of inquiry and the white paper issued on the report by the 1st respondent, which is the main complaint of the appellant in his action against the respondents, as a result of him being asked to refund N2 million or forfeit his personal assets. For this reason, I entirely agree with the court below that the trial Federal High Court lacks jurisdiction to hear and determine the appellant's action as brought before that court. This being the position, the court below also was the right in sending the case to the High Court of Kwara State, which has the necessary jurisdiction to hear and determine all the claims of the appellant," per **Mohammad JSC**.

Borderline Cases Involving Agencies of the Federal Government

1.33. For the legal practitioner, the first consideration of venue between the Federal High Court and the State High Court in matters involving the Federal Government or any agency of the Federal Government is the Federal High Court.

The reason is clearly because of the provision of section 251(1) (p) (q) (r) of the constitution which requires that the Federal High Court shall have exclusive jurisdiction in respect of suits touching and concerning the administration or management and control of the federal government or any of its agencies or interpretation of the constitution in so far as it affects them, or any actions affecting the validity of administrative actions of the Federal Government or its agencies.

1.34. The case of *Unity line Plc v. Usman* [29] is instructive. The brief fact of the above case is that, the respondent a lawyer, instituted the case for specific performance and breach of contract against the appellant, an agency of the Federal Government. The subject matter was for a simple contract, in respect of professional services. This subject matter was obviously not covered by the list of items under section 251 of the constitution. The Court of Appeal held thus:

> Since the Federal High Court has no jurisdiction to entertain the case as it did, the whole proceeding is declared a nullity," per **Adamu JCA.**

1.35. Similarly, in an action against the Kaduna Petrochemical Refining Company Limited, an agency of the Federal Government, the plaintiff sued for a simple contract;

Akitan JSC held to the effect that S. 230(1) of the 1979 Constitution, as amended by section 230(1) of decree No. 107 of 1993, which is *impari material* with section 251(1) of the 1999 Constitution, effectively provides a limitation to the jurisdiction of the Federal High Court because, the items not listed thereunder, cannot be determined by the

29 (2014) 16 NWLR (Pt. 1404) P. 546 at 552-553 Para. C-B

Federal High Court. All other items not included in the list would therefore, still be within the jurisdiction of the State High Court.

See *Onuorah v. Kaduna Refining and Petrochemical Company Limited* [30]. In the above case, the appellant entered into a contract to purchase a specific number of empty tins from the respondent, an agency of the Federal Government, at an agreed amount and payment of the agreed sum was made. But before delivery was made to the appellant, the respondent had increased the price. The appellant was duly informed of the new price and was requested to pay the difference between what he had paid and the new unit price. The appellant refused, insisting that the respondent was bound to deliver to him the quantity he had ordered at the price agreed by the parties. The main question resolved by the Supreme Court was the jurisdiction of the trial Federal High Court to entertain the suit wherein the respondent was an agency of the Federal Government. It was held per **Akitan JSC,** thus:

> In the instant case, since dispute founded on contract are not among those included in the additional jurisdiction conferred on the Federal High Court, that court therefore, had no jurisdiction to entertain the appellant's claim. The lower court, therefore, acted rightly in its decision that the Federal High Court lacked jurisdiction to entertain the claim

30 (2005) 6 NWLR (Pt. 921) P. 393 at 552-553 Para. C-B

Borderline Cases Involving Land Disputes

1.36. In the case of *Dosumu v. NNPC* (31). The applicant brought an action against Nigeria National Petroleum Company (NNPC), an agency of the Federal Government over trespass to land. **Saulawa JCA** held thus:

> As there is nothing in these sections 39, 41 and 42 of the Land Use Act that conferred any jurisdiction on the Federal High Court to entertain land case or matters, I entirely agree with the court below that the Federal High Court has no jurisdiction to hear and determine any dispute on declaration of title to land. See *Adetayo v. Ademola* (2010) LPELR- 155 SC at 23-24 (2010) 5 NWLR (Pt. 1215) page 169 at 191–192, per **Mahmud Mohammed JSC**.

1.37. "The court (High Court of Justice, Lagos State) had original jurisdiction to the exclusion of the Federal High Court to entertain the action which is rooted in trespass to land coupled with a claim for perpetual injunction in respect of the disputed piece of land," per **Ikyegh JCA.** See *Dosumu v. NNPC* (32)

1.38 Borderline Cases Involving Simple Contracts

The Federal High Court lacks jurisdiction over disputes based on simple contract. In the case of *KLM Royal Dutch Airlines v. Taher* (33) the appellate court held thus:

> The respondent had not boarded the aircraft when

31. (2014) 6 NWLR (Pt. 1403) pg. 282 at 310 Para. E-G
32. (2014) 6 NWLR (Pt. 1403) pg. 282 at 318 Para. G-H.
33. (2014) 3 NWLR (Pt. 1393) pg.137 at 193-194 Para. 4-3

the harm complained of took place. The harm was not connected with the aircraft itself; so, embarkation had not started, carriage by the aircraft had not begun... Even though the contract had been entered into, the execution of the same had not begun. At that stage, it was a simple contract between the parties, for the respondent to be carried by the 1st appellant ... for the jurisdiction of the Federal High Court to be invoked, there must have been a carriage of the passenger or the goods by the airline.

1.39. "The Federal High Court has nothing totally to do with the contract of the sale of shares", per **Bage JCA** in *Gbagi v. Okpoko* (34).

Borderline Cases Involving Law of Tort

1.38. The Federal High Court has been held to lack jurisdiction to adjudicate over tortuous liability see the case of, *KLM Royal Dutch Airline v. Taher* (35) where it was held thus:

The jurisdiction is quite circumscribed and it certainly does not include claims for damages for defamation, assaults, battery, malicious falsehood, etc.

They are all tortuous acts against a person or, to some extent, against a corporate personality and they are visibly outside the parameters of section 251 of the 1999 Constitution and therefore should not be

34. (2014) 4 NWLR (Pt. 1396) pg. 136 at 156 Para. E
35. (2014) 3 NWLR (Pt. 1393) (pg. 137) Pp. 194 Para. E-G.

entertained by the Federal High Court", per **Orji Abadua JCA.**

1.40. In the case of *Society Bic S.A. v. Charzin Industries Limited* [36] it was held thus:

> Since the claims are for libel and injunction, the State High Court and not the Federal High Court has jurisdiction to hear the claim.

36 (2014) 4 NWLR (Pt. 1398) pg. 497 at 541 Para. F-H

CHAPTER 3

When to Raise the Issue of Jurisdiction

1.40. "It is the law that the issue of jurisdiction is a threshold issue which could be raised at any stage of the proceeding and by any party even in the Supreme Court for the first time. No leave is required. It could be raised by the court, suo motu" See *FGN v. Shobu* (35)

1.41. "Objection to jurisdiction ought to be taken at the earliest opportunity, if there are sufficient materials before the court to consider it and a decision reached on it before any other step in the proceedings is taken," per **Uwaifo JSC** in *NDIC v. CBN*(36)

1.42. "The importance of jurisdiction is the reason why it can be raised at any stage of a case, be it at the trial, on appeal to the court of appeal or to this court, *afortiori,* the court can *suo motu* raise it. It is desirable that preliminary objection be raised early on issue of jurisdiction, but once it is apparent to any party that the court may not have

35. (2014) 4 NWLR (Pt. 1396) pg.45 at 59 Para. B-C
36. SC 55/1999. (2002) 7NWLR (Pt. 766) page 272

jurisdiction, it can be raised even viva voce as in this case" per **Belgore JSC** in *Petrojessica Enterprises Ltd v. Leventis Technical Co. Ltd* [(37)].

1.43. "The issue of jurisdiction is a threshold one which this court in *Elugbe v. Omokhafe* (2004) 11 12 sc 60 p. 319 held:

> must not be treated lightly......... this explains the principle of law which allows the issue of jurisdiction to be raised orally and even for the first time in this court," per **M.D Muhammad JSC** in *Salisu v Mobolaji* [(38)].

Jurisdiction to be treated first

1.44. "Jurisdiction is so fundamental that once the court's jurisdiction to hear a matter is challenged, it must be dealt with and resolved first, before any other step in the proceedings," per **Kekere-Ekun JSC** in *APGA v. Anyanwu*[(39)].

1.45. "It is basic that jurisdiction is fundamental in the adjudicatory process whenever it is raised as herein, it should be determined at the earliest opportunity. If a court has no jurisdiction to hear and determine a case, the proceedings remain a nullity ab initio," per **Fabiyi JSC** in *Attorney General of Lagos State v. Attorney General of the Federation and 35 Ors* [(40)].

37. (1992) 5 NWLR (Pt. 224) 675 at 693
38. (2014) 4 NWLR (Part 1396) Page 1 at 20-21 Para. H-C
39. (2014) 7 NWLR (Pt. 1407) pg. 541 at 565 Para. H
40. (2014) NWLR (Pt. 1412) page 217 at 275 Para. C-D

Failure to Determine Jurisdiction First

1.46. "Any failure by the court to determine any preliminary objection or any form of challenge to its jurisdiction is a fundamental breach which renders further steps taken in the proceedings a nullity," per **Rhodes-Vivour JSC** in *Obiuweubi v. CBN* [41].

When Objection to Jurisdiction Is Dismissed

1.47. The better course would have been for the trial judge to proceed with the hearing after the ruling on jurisdiction, since the ruling on jurisdiction could easily be a subject of appeal after judgment. This is clearly an unnecessary interlocutory appeal, per **Rhodes-Vivour JSC** in *Society Bic S.A. v. Charzin Industries Ltd* (2014) 4 NWLR [42]. See also *Obiuweubi v. CBN* [43]

No Jurisdiction by Consent

1.48. "Where the court lacks jurisdiction, parties cannot confer jurisdiction on the court by consent or acquiescence" per **Kekere-Ekun JSC** in *APGAv. Anyanwu* [44].

1.49. "It is obvious that no court assumes jurisdiction except it is statutorily prescribed, as jurisdiction cannot be implied nor can it be conferred by agreement of parties", per **Onnoghen JSC** *in Gafar v. Kwara State* [45].

41. (2011) 7 NWLR (Part 1247) Page 217 at 275 Para. C-D
42. (Pt. 1398) Pg 497 at 542 Para. A-D
43. (2011) All FWLR (Pt. 575) Pg. 208
44. (2014) 7 NWLR (Pt. 1407) Pg. 541 at 569 Para. A-B
45. (2007) 4 NWLR (Part 1024) Page 375 SC at 403 Para. G-H

1.50. "Finally, it must be said that neither the court nor the parties before it confer the court the jurisdiction to entertain and determine a case. Jurisdiction is statutorily conferred. In relation to courts, the issue of jurisdiction is constitutional and so a matter of law. See *Tukur v. Govt. of Gongola State* (1989) 9 SC 1, *Agbule v. Warri Refinery* and *Petrochemical Co. Limited* (2012) 12 SC 1 and *Odom v. PDP* (46)

When Objection to Jurisdiction Is Upheld

1.51. "There is no justice in exercising jurisdiction where there is none", per **Obaseki JSC** in *Oloha v. Akereja*(47).

1.52. "Any default in competence is fatal; for the proceedings are a nullity however well conducted and decided", per **Bairamian FJ** *in* the case of *Madukolu v. Nkemdilim* (48).

1.53. "The proper order following the lack of jurisdiction finding is the striking out of the suit. See *Okoye v. Nigerian Construction & Furniture Co.* (1991) 6 NWLR (Pt. 199) P401, *Central Bank of Nigeria v. Katto* (1994) 4 NWLR (Pt. 339) 446....... I make an order striking out the suit for lack of jurisdiction in the court to entertain it", per **Uwaifo JSC** in *Nigeria Deposit Insurance Corporation v. Central Bank of Nigeria* (49)

46. (2015) 6 NWLR (Pt. 1024) Pg. 527 at 566 Para. A.
47. (1988) 7SC (Pt 11) at 11-12.
48. (1962) 1 ALL NLR 587
49. (2002) 3SC Pg. 1; (2002) 7 NWLR (Pt 766) Page 272 at 300 Para. E-G

1.54. "Once a court lacks jurisdiction, a party cannot use any statutory provision or common law principle to impose it because absence of jurisdiction is irreparable in law. The matter ends there: while the only procedural duty of the court in the circumstance is to strike it out" per **Adekeye JSC** in *Obiuweubi v. Central Bank of Nigeria*[(50)].

---

50. (2011) ALL FWLR (Pt. 575) Page 208 at 240 Para. G-H

CHAPTER 4

Material for Ascertaining the Existence or Absence of Jurisdiction

1.55. It has become firmly established by a long generation of Supreme Court authorities with increasing clarity, that the yardstick for determining the jurisdiction in any matter is the claim endorsed on the writ or endorsed on the statement of claim. The Supreme Court said as much in *Adetayo v. Ademola* [51] when it held thus:

> As to what determines the jurisdiction of a court, it is now firmly settled that the jurisdiction of a court is determined by the plaintiff's claim i.e. by the subject matter and the claim before the court", per **Ogbuagu JSC.**

1.56. "Jurisdiction is determined by the plaintiff's claim and not the defence or any other process. It is the writ of summons and the statement of claim which contains the claim before the court that has to be examined in detail, to ascertain whether it comes within the jurisdiction conferred on the court by the constitution or/and statute.

51. (2010) 15 NWLR (Pt. 1215) Pg. 169 Pp 198-199 Para. G-H

See *Adeyemi v. Opeyori* (1976) 9–10 SC p.3, *PDP v. T. Sylva & 2 Ors* (2012) All FWLR (Pt. 1316) p. 85", per **Rhodes-Vivour JSC** in *Society BIC S.A. v. Charzin Industries Ltd.* (52)

1.57. "To expatiate, it can safely be said that jurisdiction is determined by what the plaintiff is demanding and cannot be a situation where the response that is anticipated, if I may say so, would be the decider", per **Mary Peter-Odili JSC** *in Society BIC S.A. v. Charzin Industries Ltd.* (53)

1.58. From the above dicta of the learned jurists of the Supreme Court, it is clear that: "The law is well settled that it is the relief or the claim in the originating process that determines the jurisdiction of the court", per **Ogunbiyi JSC** in *Okorocha v. PDP* (54).

1.59. Indeed, the Supreme Court held that: "It is a misconception for learned counsel for the appellant, to refer to facts pleaded in the statement or averments in the affidavit as components of the cause of action to be cause of action relied on in ascertaining the jurisdiction of the court", per **Ngwuta JSC** in *Society BIC S.A. v. Charzin Industries Ltd.* (55)

1.60. The above position of the law notwithstanding, it is impracticable for the court, when confronted with an

52. (2014) 4 NWLR (Pt. 1398) Page 497 Pp 538 Para. D-E
53. (2014) 4 NWLR (Pt. 1398) 497 at 551 Para. G-H.
54. (2014) 7 NWLR (Pt. 1406) Pg. 213 at 273 Para E-G
55. (2014) 4 NWLR (Pt. 1398) 497 at 535 Para. B-C.

application to strike out a suit for want of jurisdiction to completely ignore or turn a blind eye on the processes or pleadings filed by the party challenging the competence of the court to entertain the action. The court simply bears the claim in mind, while considering the objection. In the case of *Yar'adua v. Yandoma* (2015) 4 NWLR (Pt. 1448) page 123 (at 161 Para. C-H), **M. D. Muhammad JSC** held thus:

> This court has, in a prethora of cases, provided the procedure to guide the courts in the determination of the issue of their competence where same is raised. In *Lado v. CPC* (supra) which we all seem to be obsessed with in the matter at hand, this Court at page 724 of the report, per **Onnoghen JSC** has stated the procedure broadly thus:
>
> While it is settled law that it is the claim of a plaintiff as evidenced in the writ of summons and statement of claim that determines the jurisdiction of the court where however, from the totality of the pleadings of both parties and the evidence adduced to establish same, it becomes obvious that the court has no jurisdiction with regards to the subject matter of the dispute or that the claim, in reality, cannot come within the statutory jurisdiction of the court, the court will take into account the totality of the facts pleaded by the parties and the evidence adduced to establish the same in determining whether the court has jurisdiction or not."
>
> The procedure to adopt, where an objection is raised to the jurisdiction of the court in a matter

> commenced by originating summons, is to consider the objection together with the substantive matter. Invariably, this would involve the consideration of not only the reliefs being claimed against the background of the facts deposed to in the affidavit in support of the originating summons but the totality of available evidence including the facts contained in the counter-affidavit(s) in opposition to the originating summons. See *Adeleke v. OSHA* (2006) 16 NWLR (Pt. 1096) 508, *Amadi v. NNPC* (2000) 10 NWLR (Pt. 674) 75 at 100 and *Dapilalong v. Dariye* (supra).

In the resolution of the jurisdictional issue this appeal raises therefore, the materials to examine in relation to the decisions of the two courts below are 1st–10th respondents originating summons, their affidavits in support of same as well as the counter-affidavits of the defendants in the suit that brought about the instant appeal."

Law Governing Jurisdiction vs Law Governing Cause of Action

1.61. "The law in force or existing at the time the cause of action arose is the law applicable for determining the case. This law does not necessarily determine the jurisdiction of the court at the time the jurisdiction is involved. That is to say, the law in force at the time cause of action arose, governs the determinate of the suit. While the law in force at the time of trial, based on the case of action, determines the court vested with jurisdiction to try the case, per **Rhodes-vivour JSC,** in *Obiuweubi v. CBN*(56).

In the above case, it was also held that "the jurisdiction of the Federal High Court to entertain an action is determined by examinig the law conferring jurisdiction at the time the suit was instituted and trial commenced"(57)

Jurisdiction on Appeal

1.62. "It is trite that there are exceptions to the general rule that the leave of court must be sought and obtained before raising an issue not decided by the lower court. The exception, are where the new issue(s) borders on jurisdiction, leave need not be obtained", per **Uwa J.C.A** in *F.G.N v. Shobu (Nig.) Limited.* (58)

Fate of Appeal where Trial Court Lacked Jurisdiction

1.63. "The jurisdiction of the lower court to entertain the appeal was dependant upon the jurisdiction of the trial court to hear and determine the suit before it, in the first instance. The importance of this issue was well illustrated in a recent decision of this court in *SLB Consortium Limited v. NNPC* (2011) 9 NWLR (Pt. 1252) Page 317 at 567", per **Kekere-Ekun JSC** in *APGA v. Anyanwu*(59).

56. (2011) All NWLR (Pt. 575) Page 208 at 230 Para. G-H page 231 Para. A
57. Rhodes-Vivour JSC at 231 Para. C.
58. (2014) 4 NWLR (Pt. 1396) page 45 at 58 Para. G-H.
59. (2014) 7 NWLR (Pt. 1407) pg. 541 at 567 Para. G-H.

1.64. "If the trial court lacks jurisdiction to entertain the case, its proceedings are a nullity and the lower court would have no jurisdiction to entertain the appeal arising therefrom. Whether or not the appellant has suffered a miscarriage of justice by the omission of the lower court does not arise, the issue of jurisdiction raised in this case, being one of substantive law", per **Kekere-Ekun JSC** [60].

60. (2014) 7 NWLR (Pt. 1407) Page 541 Pp. 568-569 Para H - A

PART 2

CHAPTER 5

Section 251 (1) (A) – (O) of the 1999 Constitution through the Cases

The objective of this part is to review cases which deal with the provisions of section 251(1) of the 1999 Constitution. The exclusive jurisdiction of the Federal High Court under the constitution, constitute direct issues for determination in the cases reviewed. The focus is on those *ratio decidendi* in appellate decisions, which boils down to a consideration of the jurisdiction of the Federal High Court as against the State High Courts over subject matters itemised under section 251(1)(a)-(o) of the 1999 Constitution, spanning various circumstances. As all practitioners know, no two cases have exactly the same set of facts and circumstances. However, the cases considered herein, go far afield enough, to chart a path into the mind of the appellate courts while deciding the interplay of multiple combinations of legal factors as they affect the jurisdiction of both courts.

REVENUE OF THE FEDERAL GOVERNMENT S. 251(1)(a)

IN THE COURT OF APPEAL
(Kaduna Judicial Division)

Suit No: CA/K/14/98

A.M. SHITTU v. NIGERIAN AGRICULTURAL & COOPERATIVE BANK LIMITED & ORS

Citation: (2001) 10 NWLR (Pt. 721) 298

Date: Wednesday the 14th day of June, 2000

FACTS

The 1st respondent as plaintiff before the Federal High Court, Kano Division claimed in its writ of summons as follows:

(i) A declaration that the action of the defendants in closing and sealing of offices of the plaintiff at Dutse and Hadejia is an unauthorised method of enforcing tax liabilities if any, of the plaintiff and therefore illegal, unconstitutional, null and void.

(ii) An injunction restraining the defendants, privies or whosoever acting on their instruction, from sealing and closing the offices of the plaintiff, in purported enforcing of alleged tax liabilities of the plaintiff to the defendant.

A motion for interlocutory injunction was filed by the

plaintiff and granted by the court. The 3rd defendant now the appellant filed a preliminary objection by a motion on notice, dated 11/6/97, praying the court as follows:

(i) an order striking out the plaintiff's claim for want of jurisdiction;

(ii) an order discharging the order of interlocutory injunction granted on 20th of May, 1997;

(iii) an order awarding damages to the defendants.

The motion was heard by the learned trial judge. In his ruling, the learned trial judge dismissed the application of the 3rd defendant/appellant and held that he had jurisdiction to hear and determine the matter. The 3rd defendant/appellant was not satisfied with the decision and therefore, he appealed against same before the Court of Appeal.

ISSUE FOR DETERMINATION

Whether the Federal High Court, Kano Division can properly assume jurisdiction as it did over the plaintiff/ respondent's claim which bothers on Personal Income Tax, a revenue accruable to Jigawa State Government?

HELD

1. "There is no provision conferring jurisdiction on the Federal High Court to try any civil cases or matters connected with or pertaining to the revenue of the government of a state or any authority established

by the government of a state", per **Obadina, JCA** at 314, para. F

2. "A critical look at the provisions of Decree No. 60 of 1991 and section 230(1) of the 1979 Constitution as amended by Decree No. 107 of 1993 (Now s. 251(1) (a) of the 1999 constitution), seems to show that the gravamen of the jurisdiction of the Federal High Court concerns matters connected with or pertaining to the revenue of the Government of the Federation, as may be spelt out by the National Assembly", per **Obadina, JCA** page 316, para. A-B

In the Court of Appeal of Nigeria

Abuja Judicial Division

CA/A/89/2013

HONOURABLE FAROUK LAWAN v. ZENON PETROLEUM & GAS LIMITED & ORS

Citation: (2014) LPELR-23206(CA)

Date: Friday, the 13th day of June, 2014

FACTS

This is an appeal against the ruling of the High Court of the Federal Capital Territory, Abuja Judicial Division (**Coram U. P. Kekemeke, J**) in suit No. FCT/HC/CV/3839/2012 delivered on the 30th day of January, 2013. In the ruling, the High Court of the Federal Capital Territory (hereinafter referred to as "the lower court") dismissed the preliminary objection of the appellant which sought a striking out or dismissal of the suit.

A summary of the facts forming the background of this appeal is as follows: by a resolution of the House of Representatives made on 8th January 2012, an ad hoc committee of the said House was set up to verify and determine the actual subsidy requirement and monitor the implementation of the petroleum subsidy regime in Nigeria. The appellant was the head of the ad hoc committee. The 2nd respondent (the chairman of the 1st respondent) claimed that the appellant contacted him, informing him that the 1st respondent was going to be indicted by his committee for purchasing foreign exchange from the Central Bank of Nigeria without importing petroleum products, unless the 1st and 2nd respondents paid a bribe of US $3,000,000:00 (three million United States dollars). In spite of the 2nd respondent's, explanations, the appellant persisted in making calls to the 2nd respondent, calculated to intimidate the 1st and 2nd respondents, to meet his demand.

On the 18th day of April 2012, the appellant presented the report of his committee before the 3rd respondent indicting, inter alia, the 1st respondent. Following alleged continuous harassments by the appellant and on the advice of security agencies, the 1st and 2nd respondents variously handed over to the appellant and another person, marked currency notes totaling US $620,000 (Six hundred and twenty thousand United States dollars). After the name of the 1st respondent, was said to have been delisted from the list of indicted companies, the appellant allegedly persisted in making phone calls to the 1st and 2nd respondents, for them to pay up the balance of the sum of money allegedly demanded. The 1st and 2nd respondents further alleged that the 3rd respondent and another person conspired to relist the 1st respondent with the aim of intimidating them to drop their complaints against the appellant and 3rd respondent to the police. On account of the above allegations, the 1st and 2nd respondents sued the appellant, 3rd respondent and two others, viz; the clerk of the National Assembly and the National Assembly at the lower court claiming the following reliefs:

1. the sum of N100,000,000,000 (one hundred billion naira), against the defendants as general damages for the acts of intimidation, loss of goodwill and patronage occasioned by the acts of the defendants.

2. the sum of N150,000,000,000 (one hundred and fifty billion naira), against the defendant as exemplary damages for their oppressive and arbitrary action.

Upon the receipt of the originating process the appellant entered a conditional appearance and filed a notice of preliminary objection, challenging the jurisdiction of the court to entertain the suit and/or the competence of the suit. Before the preliminary objection was argued, the 1st and 2nd respondents discontinued the action against the clerk of the National Assembly and the National Assembly ,at the lower court. Their names were accordingly struck out of the suit. After taking arguments from both sides, the lower court, as earlier stated, dismissed the preliminary objection.

Aggrieved by the ruling, the appellant filed a notice of appeal containing nine grounds of appeal.

ISSUE FOR DETERMINATION

Whether or not the lower court was right to have assumed jurisdiction to entertain this matter, having regard to the provision of section 251 of the Constitution of the Federal Republic of Nigeria, 1999 (as amended)?

HELD

1. "It is however my view that where any of such persons is alleged to have acted outside the limit or bounds of his authority or in his private pursuit, he cannot claim to be acting as an agent of the government of the federation or bind the government in such a circumstance. See *Azubuike v. Government of Enugu State* (2014) 5 NWLR (1400) 364, 392. In the instant case, the appellant is alleged to have used the occasion of his being the head of a committee of the House of Representatives to continuously harass and intimidate the 1st and 2nd respondents to part with a bribe of US $3,000,000 (three million United States dollars). The 3rd respondent is alleged to have sought to intimidate the 1st and 2nd respondents to drop their complaints against them, by conspiring with another to relist the name of the 1st respondent on the list of companies indicted by the ad hoc committee headed by the appellant. Going by the above, it is my view and I agree with counsel for the 1st and 2nd respondents that, neither the appellant nor the 3rd respondent can be classified as agents or organs of the Government of the Federation in this instance. In the case of *Akegbejo v. Ataga* (1998) 1 NWLR (534) 459, 467, this court held that a State High Court has no jurisdiction where agents of the Federal Government are sued in their official capacities in respect of the executive or administrative actions of the Federal Government or its agency. This is not so in this case. Indeed,

counsel for the appellant noted in his brief that the appellant was not sued in his capacity as the chairman of the ad hoc committee", per **Ekanem, JCA.**

2. "To bring a suit under the exclusive jurisdiction of the Federal High Court in section 251(1)(a) and (r) of the Constitution, the suit must relate to the revenue of the Government of the Federation or the action must be for a declaration or injunction affecting the validity of an executive or administrative action or decision by the Federal Government or any of its agencies.

The Federal High Court is not seized with jurisdiction to adjudicate over tort, no matter the parties involved, as tort does not fall into any of the provisions of section 251 of the constitution. It is only the High Court of the Federal Capital Territory or of a state that has jurisdiction in such a matter. I draw strength for this position from the following cases; *Oamen v. Owenan* (1993) 8 NWLR (311) 358, 368, *Tanarewa (Nigeria) Ltd v. Arzai* (2005) 5 NWLR (Pt. 919) 593, 642 and *Hallmark Bank Plc v. Obasanjo* (2014) 4 NWLR (1397) 209, 222 and 224. This case, as crafted in the writ of summons and statement of claim, has nothing to do with the revenue of the government of the federation nor does it affect the validity of an executive or administrative action or decision of the Federal Government or its agency.

"Revenue of the Government of the Federation" refers to the income which the Federal Government collects and receives into its treasury, and is appropriate for the payment of its expenses. See Black's Law Dictionary, 5th Ed. p. 1185. The demand allegedly made, did not contemplate payment into or out of the treasury of the Government of the Federation", per **Ekanem, JCA**.

In The Court of Appeal of Nigeria

Enugu Judicial Division

CA/E/31/2005

NZUBE ANAZODO v. PAZMECK INTER TRADE, NIGERIA & ANOR

Citation: (2008) 6 *NWLR* (Pt. 1084) Page 529

Date: Thursday, the 14th day of June, 2007

FACTS

This is an appeal against the judgment of Nnewi High Court in Anambra State of Nigeria, delivered on the 27th day of July, 2004 in Suit No. HN/124/2001: Pazmeek Inter-trade Nig. Ltd and 1 other and Nzube Anazodo. By paragraph 15 of the amended statement of claim, the plaintiffs (now respondents), sued the defendant (now appellant), for the sum of five million naira, being special and general damages caused to the plaintiffs by the wrongful act of the defendant, alleged to have been paid to facilitate custom and excise processes in respect of imported goods.

In a considered judgment, the learned trial judge substantially granted the claim and dismissed the counterclaim of the defendant of N200,000.00, being the balance of the agreed fee of N900,000.00 not paid. Dissatisfied with the above decision, the appellant now appealed to the Court of Appeal.

ISSUE FOR DETERMINATION

Whether the holding by the learned trial judge that the State High Court has jurisdiction to entertain this suit, in spite of the issues pertaining to the revenue of the Government of the Federation and operations of Nigerian Customs Service, inextricably interwoven in the subject-matter of the appeal was correct, in view of the provisions of section 251 of the 1999 Constitution of Nigeria?

HELD

1. "In order to appreciate the arguments of the learned counsel for the parties, it would be necessary to set out section 251(1)(a) and (c) of the 1999 Constitution of the Federal Republic of Nigeria and it is as follows:

   "251(1) Notwithstanding anything to the contrary contained in this constitution and in addition to such other jurisdiction as may be conferred upon it by an Act of the National Assembly, the Federal High Court shall have and exercise jurisdiction to the exclusion of any other court in civil cases and matters:

   (a) relating to the revenue of the Government of the Federation in which the said Government or any organ thereof or a person suing or being sued on behalf of the said government is a party;

   (b) connected with or pertaining to customs and excise duties and export duties, including any claim by or against the Nigeria Customs Service or any member or officer thereof, arising from the performance of any duty imposed under any regulation relating to customs and excise duties and export duties.

A perusal of the said section 251(1)(a) and (c) of the Constitution quoted above envisages a civil case or matter relating to the revenue of the Government of the Federation in which the said government or an organ thereat or a person suing or being sued on behalf of the Federal Government is a party. In the instant case, neither the Federal Government nor any of its organs or agencies was a party to the suit in the lower court. The case of the respondents/cross appellants was based on losses suffered by them as a result of wrongdoing on the part of the appellant, and mere reference to the board of Customs is not the same as a claim by or against the Nigerian Customs Service.

In *Jammal Steel Structures Limited v. African Continental Bank Limited* (1973) 1 All NLR (Pt. II) page 208, the Supreme Court considered and interpreted section 9(1) of the Federal High Court Act, No. 23 of 1973 which is about the same with section 251(1)(a) of the 1999 Constitution of the Federal Republic of Nigeria and held among others that:

> for the Federal High Court to have exclusive jurisdiction, two conditions must be fulfilled
>
> (i) the case or matter must relate to the revenue of the Federation or its organs or agencies;
>
> (ii) the Federal Government or its agency must be a party", per **Bada, JCA,** pp. 541-542, para. B-C.

2. "There was nothing in the action before the lower court to suggest or indicate that the revenue of the Federal Government was involved or that the Federal Government or any of its organs was a party to the suit. The mere mention of or reference to the board of customs, payment of custom duties, seizure and detention of the container by the board of Customs as a result of forging of the Clean Report of Inspection and investigation of the forgery by the board of customs and subsequent release of the container to the respondents are not sufficient to oust the jurisdiction of the State High Court on ordinary matter of breach of contract or tort, more so when the action in question is not a claim by or against Nigeria Customs Service" per **Bada, JCA,** p. 542, para. C-E.

IN THE SUPREME COURT OF NIGERIA

SC.20/2008

THE HONOURABLE ATTORNEY GENERAL OF LAGOS STATE v. THE HONOURABLE ATTORNEY GENERAL OF THE FEDERATION & ORS

Citation: (2014) 7 NWLR (pt. 1412) Page 217

Date: On Friday, the 11th day of April, 2014

FACT

By an amended originating summons filed before the Supreme Court, seeking to invoke its original jurisdiction on the 12th day of August, 2009, the plaintiff's claims against the defendants thus:

> That the House of Assembly of Lagos State of Nigeria is the body entitled, to the exclusion of any other legislative body, to enact laws with regards to the imposition and collection of tax on the supply of all goods and services within Lagos State of Nigeria and that Lagos State of Nigeria, or any agency of the State, is the body entitled, to the exclusion of any other body, to assess and collect such tax, and that the revenue of the Lagos State Government has been and continues to be affected by the enforcement of the provisions of the Value Added Tax Act Cap VI, Laws of the Federal Republic of Nigeria, 2004 (hereinafter referred to as the 'VAT Act'.

On determining the questions set out in the summons, the plaintiff prays the court for the following reliefs:

(1) a declaration that the Value Added Tax Act, Cap VI Laws of the Federal Republic of Nigeria 2004 is to the extent that it provides for the imposition and collection of taxes on goods and services in Lagos State (and other states of the Federation), outside the legislative competence of the National Assembly and is, therefore, unconstitutional, null and void and of no effect whatsoever.

(2) a perpetual injunction restraining the Federal Government of Nigeria by itself, its servants or any of its agencies from continuing to give effect to the provision of the said Value Added Tax Act, to impose and collect taxes on goods and services within Lagos State Nigeria.

The 1st defendant, the Attorney General of the Federation, upon being served the amended originating summons, the supporting affidavit and the exhibits annexed thereto, on 3rd February, 2010, filed a Notice of Preliminary Objection pursuant to Order 2 Rule 29 of the Supreme Court Rules, 2002 and section 232 (1) of the Constitution of the Federal Republic of Nigeria, 1999, urging the court to strike out and/or dismiss the plaintiff's suit.

ISSUE FOR DETERMINATION

Whether there is a dispute between the Lagos State Government and the Federation in respect of the constitutionality of the Value Added Tax Act as it applies to Lagos State (as well as other states of the federation) over which the Supreme Court may exercise exclusive jurisdiction?

HELD

On the Status of the specific Jurisdiction of the Federal High Court

1. "The specific jurisdiction vested in the Federal High Court under section 251(1)(a), (b) and (q) is exercisable "notwithstanding anything to the contrary in the constitution" including the original jurisdiction conferred on the Supreme Court under the earlier section 232 (1) of the same constitution", per **Muhammad, JSC** at 259, para. D-E.

On Jurisdiction to Interprete S.251 of the Constitution

2. "The plaintiff, whose claim clearly relates to the revenue of the Government of the Federation, consequent upon the taxes one of its agencies levies and/or seeks the interpretation of the constitution as to how the operation of the constitution affects the 1st defendant or any of its agencies, is at the wrong court. This court must decline jurisdiction. I so hold", per **Muhammad, JSC** at 261, para. B-C.

FEDERAL TAXATION S.251(1)(b)

In the Court of Appeal

Ibadan Judicial Division

Suit No: CA/I/209/98

ELF OIL NIGERIA LIMITED v. OYO STATE BOARD OF INTERNAL REVENUE

Citation:

Other citation: (2002) LPELR-12260(CA)

Date: On Thursday, the 18th day of April, 2002

FACTS

By an originating summons dated the 17/2/98 issued at the Ibadan Division of the High Court of Oyo State, the respondent claimed against the appellant herein:

A. Declaration that by virtue of the combined provisions of Section 96 of the Personal Income Tax Decree (PITD) No. 104 of 1993 and section 28 of Oyo State Internal Revenue Board Amended Edict 1997, the applicant is empowered to distrain the respondent of its goods, chattels, land and/or premises, etc., for non-payment of Business Premises Registration/Renewal Rates levy and tax being unremitted deduction in respect of PAYE and W.H.T. under the said law.

B. An order distraining the respondent of its goods,

chattels, lands, premises, etc. for non-payment of N4,852,319.00 (four million eight hundred and fifty-two thousand three hundred and nineteen naira only), being outstanding levy and tax payable by the respondent to the applicant under the Business Premises Registration/Renewal Rates, Pay as You Earn (PAYE) deductions and Withholding Taxes for the years 1991-1996, until the settlement of the tax liability.

C. And for such further order or orders as this Honourable Court may deem fit to make in the circumstances.

To this, the appellant filed a Notice of Preliminary Objection. The learned trial judge gave his ruling wherein the preliminary objection was dismissed. The present appeal is against that ruling.

One of the grounds of appeal is to wit:

> the learned trial judge erred in law in holding that he has jurisdiction to try this case, when jurisdiction on the taxation of companies and other bodies established or carrying on businesses in Nigeria and all other persons subject to federal taxation has been exclusively vested in the Federal High court by virtue of the Federal High Court Amendment Decree No. 60 of 1991 with effect from 26th August 1993. Therefore, Oyo State Internal Revenue Board (Amendment) Edict No. 12 of 1997 which empowers the State High Court to exercise

jurisdiction in this case is inconsistent with the said Decree 60 of 1991 and, therefore, null and void and of no effect whatsoever.

ISSUE FOR DETERMINATION

Whether the Oyo State High Court has jurisdiction to try this case, in view of the provisions of Section 7(i)(b)(ii) and 8(i) of the Federal High Court Act Cap. 134 Laws of the Federation of Nigeria, 1990?

HELD

1. "With respect to the 3rd issue, section 2(2) of the Personal Income Tax Decree No. 104 of 1993 provides:

   In the case of (an) individuals, other than an itinerant worker and persons covered under paragraph (b) of subsection (1) of this section, tax for any year of assessment may be imposed only by the state in which the individual is deemed to be resident for that year under the provisions of the First Schedule to this Decree and in the case of persons referred to in subsection (1)(b) of this section, tax shall be imposed by the Federal Board of Internal Revenue."

   This provision clearly shows that a state is authorised to impose tax on individuals deemed to be resident therein other than those mentioned in paragraph (b) of subsection (1) of section 2 and itinerant workers", per **Tabai, JCA.**

2. "The result, therefore, is that there is nothing so far to show that the respondent is not entitled to the amounts claimed in respect of the 1993, 1994, 1995 and 1996 years of assessment under the Personal Income Tax Decree No. 104 of 1993; nor is there so far anything to show that the amounts claimed fall within matters under the exclusive jurisdiction of the Federal High Court as provided in sections 7(1)(b)(ii) and 8(1) of the Federal High Court Act Cap. 134 Laws of the Federation of Nigeria 1990. I hold in conclusion, therefore, that there are, so far, no materials to establish that the High Court of Oyo State has no jurisdiction to entertain the suit", per **Tabai, JCA.**

In the Court of Appeal of Nigeria

CA/L/241/2009

LAGOS STATE INTERNAL REVENUE BOARD v. MOTOROLA NIGERIA LIMITED

Citation: (2012) LPELR-14712(CA)

Date: On Friday, the 1st day of June, 2012

FACTS

The 1st respondent as plaintiff commenced an action in the lower court by writ of summons and in paragraph 17 of the statement of claim sought for the following reliefs:

a) A declaration that the defendant acted unlawfully in sealing up the offices of the plaintiff on 18th September, 2008 in purport enforcement of the defendant's notice of tax assessment, dated 4th April 2008 and referenced as LA/IRS/SDLM/COLL/DN/MN453703/08 when the plaintiff had served on the defendant on the 3rd of September, 2008, a notice of appeal against the rejection by the defendant of the plaintiff's objection to the assessment.

b) An injunction restraining the 2nd defendant from honouring, upon presentation of the cheque, dated 18th September, 2008, issued by the plaintiff in favour of the 1st defendant in consequence of the sealing up by the 1st defendant of the offices of the plaintiff, amounting to the sum of N90,649,092.96.

c) An order of perpetual injunction, restraining the 1st defendant or its agent from further harassing, intimidating and disrupting the business of the plaintiff in any way or form. In the alternative, an order that, pending the determination of the appeal pursuant to the notice of appeal dated 3rd September, 2008, the defendant refunds to the plaintiff the sum of N90,649,092.96 paid to it by the plaintiff on 18th September, 2008, consequent upon the sealing up of the offices of the plaintiff by the defendant.

d) Special damages against the 1st defendant at the rate of 21% per annum on the sum of N90,649,092.96 from the date the said sum of N90,649,092.96 leaves the plaintiff's bank account until the day it is refunded by the 1st defendant.

e) N10,000,000.00 general damages for the disruption of business and embarrassment caused the plaintiff by the unlawful action of the 1st defendant in sealing up its offices.

f) N10,000,000.00 aggravated and or exemplary damages against the 1st defendant for the disregard shown for the rule of law in sealing up of the offices of the plaintiff in disregard of a pending notice of appeal." On 22nd September, 2008, the plaintiff filed two motions - one ex-parte and the other on notice seeking for interim and interlocutory injunctions respectively, restraining the 2nd defendant from honouring upon presentation of the forty (40) cheques in the total sum of N89,624,043.30 issued by the plaintiff to the 1st defendant after the 1st defendant had distrained the plaintiff of its premises. When the 1st defendant was served with the motions, it entered a conditional appearance and later filed notice of preliminary objection to the jurisdiction of the Federal High Court to entertain the suit.

The learned trial judge overruled the objection raised. The present appeal is a fall out of the ruling of the Federal High Court, Lagos Judicial Division, delivered by the Hon. Justice Charles Efanga Archibong on November 3, 2009. By the said ruling, the lower court held that it has jurisdiction over the subject matter of the suit No. FHC/C/L/CS/5275/2008, by virtue of the provisions of the Exclusive Legislative List, item 59, part one of the Second Schedule to the Constitution of the Federal Republic of Nigeria 1999, as amended.

The notice of appeal was predicated upon a sole ground, viz:

Ground

The honourable judge erred in law when his lordship held that the court would assume jurisdiction because taxation is listed as item 59 under the Exclusive Legislative List of the Federal Republic of Nigeria, 1999.

Particulars of Appeal

1. The claim before the court is on the enforcement of

personal income tax of employee of the 1st respondent under the Pay As You Earn Scheme of the Personal Income Tax Act which is a matter under the concurrent legislative list of the Constitution of the Federal Republic of Nigeria.

2. The imposition of tax was not an issue raised either by the 1st respondent in its originating process or part of the grounds of objection arisen (sic) from the process filed by the appellant before the court.

ISSUE FOR DETERMINATION

"Whether the Federal High Court has jurisdiction to entertain and determine the present action."

HELD

1. "There is no dispute that the provisions of the 1999 Constitution give the National Assembly exclusive power to legislate on taxation of income. Section 4(2) of the Constitution provides:

   The National Assembly shall have power to make laws for the peace, order and good government of the federation or any part thereof with respect to any matter included in the Exclusive Legislative List set out in Part 1 of the Second Schedule to this Constitution.

Item 59 of the Second Schedule, part 1 lists the taxation of incomes, profits and capital gains as being covered in the Exclusive Legislative List. Even though taxation of incomes, profits and capital gains are items on the Exclusive Legislative List, the collection of taxes is brought under the Concurrent Legislative List, Specifically Item D7 says:

"In the exercise of its powers to impose any tax or duty on:

(a) capital gains, incomes or profits of persons other than companies; and

(b) documents or transactions by way of stamp duties, the National Assembly may, subject to such conditions as it may prescribe, provide that the collection of any such tax or duty or the administration of the law imposing it, shall be carried out by the Government of a state or other authority of the state", per **Akaahs, JCA**.

2. The collection of income tax mentioned in Item D7 of the Concurrent Legislative List is the constitutional responsibility of the state government. Therefore, the imposition and enforcement of Pay As You Earn of employees of companies (including those of the 1st respondent) resident in Lagos State is vested in the appellant.

It is a cardinal principle of interpretation of the constitution that the intentions of the lawmakers should be to bring them out and not to defeat the aims and objectives of the constitution. See *Nafiu Rabiu v. Kano State Government* (1980) 8-11 SC 130. And the intention in the constitution is to create a division in the administration and collection of taxes between the Federal and State

Governments. It should be emphasised that jurisdiction of a court is a matter of law and it is vested on a court by the constitution and the statute establishing the court. Under section 251 (1) (a) of the 1999 Constitution, the Federal High Court exercises jurisdiction to the exclusion of any other court in cases and matters relating to the revenue of the Government of the Federation in which the said government or any of its agencies is a party. The court under S. 251(1)(d) of the Constitution also exercises exclusive jurisdiction in civil cases and matters arising from banking, banks, other financial institutions including any action between one bank and another, any action by or against the Central Bank of Nigeria (CBN) arising from banking, foreign exchange, coinage, legal tender bills of exchange, letter of credit, promissory note and other fiscal measures. See *NDIC v. Okem Enterprises Limited* at 181-182 per **Uwaifo, JSC.**

The subject matter of this suit has nothing to do with the operation of the 1st respondent's company and even if the action is to challenge the lawfulness of the act of enforcing an alleged tax liability, it is not questioning the power of the National Assembly to make the law and since it is expressly stated that it is the State that can enforce the payment of personal income tax, the challenge should go to the State High Court.

The collection of taxes due to Lagos State Government is definitely not covered by section 251 (1) of the 1999 Constitution. See *A. M. Shittu v. Nigeria Agricultural & Cooperative Bank Limited & Ors* (2001) 10 NWLR (Pt. 721) 298; *Progressive Insurance Co. Limited v. Adepoju* (1991) 1

NWLR (Pt. 166) 248 and *Ministry of Works v. Tomas Nig. Limited* (2002) 2 NWLR (Pt. 752) 744. In *Shittu v. N.A.C.B. Limited* (supra) it was held that there is no provision expressed or implied in the Personal Income Tax Decree no. 104 of 1993 (now Act) conferring jurisdiction on the Federal High Court to hear and determine civil cases and matters connected with or pertaining to the revenue accruable to the government of a state by virtue of the provisions of the decree. The facts in the Shittu's case supra are similar to those in this appeal and the decision in that case is quite opposite to the resolution of the issue raised in this appeal," per **Akaahs, JCA.**

IN THE COURT OF APPEAL OF NIGERIA
Holding at Ibadan
CA/I/175/2006

IKENNE LOCAL GOVERNMENT v. WEST AFRICAN PORTLAND CEMENT PLC

Citation: (2012) All FWLR (pt.642) 1747

Date: On Monday, the 21st day of March, 2011

FACTS

Appellant in its writ of summons filed at the State High Court and paragraph 12 of the statement of claim claimed against the respondent as follows:

1. Declaration

(a) That defendant is in physical occupation of the non-urban, rural area parcel of land, measuring approximately 50 acres, lying and being in the vicinity of and opposite Tropical paints company along Iperu/Sagamu Road, Iperu and have been in such occupation prior to 30th September, 1998.

(b) That the land referred to in (a) above is within the territorial and administrative jurisdiction of the plaintiff.

(c) That pursuant to sections 1 & 2 of the Taxes and Levies (Approved List for Collection) Decree 1998, the plaintiff is the appropriate tax authority entitled to assess or collect occupancy fees listed as item 7 in part III of the Schedule to the Decree aforesaid, in respect of the land referred to in (a) and (b) above.

(d) That the occupancy fees assessed due and payable to the plaintiff by the defendant excludes and does not include any royalties, compensation, rent or any surface rent paid or, payable to the Federal or\and Ogun State Governments under any enactment or law.

2. Order of Court

   (a) That the defendant is liable to pay occupancy fees as assessed due and payable to the plaintiff with effect from 1st October, 1998 in respect of their occupation of the land referred to, in claim 1(a) and (b) above.

   (b) Restraining the defendant whether by itself, its servants, agents, contractors', workers', privies or otherwise, howsoever described from entering the aforesaid land or from remaining in occupation thereof until after every outstanding sum of money representing the whole or part thereof of its liability for occupancy fees as assessed with interests and penalties from 1st October 1998 to date is paid to the plaintiff

3. The sum of N36,000,000:00 (thirty-six million naira) being occupancy fees payable in respect of the defendant's occupation of the parcel of land referred to in claim 1(a) and (b) above with effect from 1st

October, 1998 to 30th September, 2004.

4. The sum of N7,560,000.00 (seven million five hundred and sixty thousand naira) being pro-rated interest on the amount in claim 3 above at the rate of 27% per annum from 1st October, 1998 to 30th September, 2004.

5. The sum of N3,600,000.00 (three million, six hundred thousand naira) being penalties due and payable on (3) above at 10% per annum.

6. Interest payable on the joint amounts claimed in claims (3), (4) and (5) above at the rate of 21% per annum with effect from 1st October, 2004 until judgment and thereafter at the rate of 60% until final payment.

The respondent defaulted in filing its statement of defence and filed application for extension of time within which to file the statement of defence. The application was granted on the 9th of November, 2005.

Before the hearing of the respondent's application for extension of time, the respondent had filed a notice of preliminary objection dated 14th October, 2005. The grounds of the objection are:

(a) that the plaintiff's suit does not disclose any reasonable cause of action and same should be struck out;

(b) that the court lacks the jurisdiction to entertain the matter;

(c) that the plaintiff's suit is not properly constituted.

At the end of the arguments before it, the lower court declined jurisdiction to entertain the appellant's case and ruled that the matter be heard before the Federal High Court. Appellant filed a notice of appeal on the 17th of May, 2006.

ISSUE FOR DETERMINATION

Whether from the contents of the writ of summons and the statement of claim filed by the appellant in this case at the lower court, it can justifiably be held that the High Court of Ogun State lacks jurisdiction to entertain, hear and determine the appellant's case against the respondent?

HELD

1. "It is apparent that the suit was for the recovery of occupancy fees. The subject matter of the appellant's case under item 7 in Part III to the Schedule to Taxes & Levies (Approved List for Collection) Decree 21 of 1998 concerns right of occupancy fees on lands in rural areas, excluding those collectable by the federal and state governments. The right of occupancy fees involved in this case is neither a tax on the profits of the respondent nor is it revenue accruing to the Federal Government. The liability to pay right of occupancy fees as rightly submitted by the appellant in its reply brief is at best a deductible expense of the company, wholly, exclusively and reasonably incurred in the course and by reason of the

respondent's occupation of the 50 acres of land within the territory and local government area of the appellant for the company's business operation in the nature of and analogous to rents incurred and payable for office premises or staff salaries or bank charges. See the cases of *Shell Dev. Co Nig. Limited v. F.B.I.R* (1996) 8 N.W.L.R Part 466 page 256 at 290-291 paragraphs B-D per Uwais CJN (as he then was) and *Gulf Oil Nig. Limited v. F.B.I.R* (1997) 7 N.W.L.R Part 514 at 698", per **Fasanmi, JCA** at p.1766 para. C - F

2. "It is clear from the above provision that section 251 (1) (b) of the 1999 Constitution is on Federal taxation of companies i.e. the tax companies are to pay to the Federal Government for operating as companies. The collection of ground rents for certificate of occupancy in respect to land is an issue under the Land Use Act. It is quite different from taxation of companies. On a close examination of the entire provision of section 251 of the 1999 Constitution, prescribing the jurisdiction of the Federal High court to the exclusion of all other courts, there is nothing specifically conferring jurisdiction on that court in cases or matters concerning land disputes. Although the section also indicates that the National Assembly may confer additional jurisdiction to the court, there is no indication that such Act of the National Assembly had been promulgated conferring additional jurisdiction to the court to entertain cases and matters on land disputes. If any such additional

jurisdiction had been given, the most relevant statute to examine is the Land Use Act because jurisdiction of the Federal High court to entertain 'occupational fees' on land matters cannot be inferred by implication in the construction of section 251 of the 1999 Constitution, the meaning of which is quite clear and plain as no cases or matters in land dispute are mentioned therein. See *Adisa v. Oyinwola* (2000) 10 NWLR Pt. 674 at 116 and *Adetayo v. Ademola* (2010) 15 NWLR Part 1215 page 169 at 204 para. D-F", per **Fasanmi, JCA** at pp. 1767-1768, para. E–A

3. "It is therefore my view that the subject matter of the appellant's action is within the jurisdiction of the High Court of Ogun State", per **Fasanmi, JCA** at p. 1768, para. C

IN THE COURT OF APPEAL OF NIGERIA

CA/A/256/2007

BAMAK PHARMACY & STORES LTD & ORS v. ABUJA MUNICIPAL AREA COUNCIL

Citation: (2010) LPELR-CA/A/256/2007

Date: On Thursday, the 18th day of March, 2010

FACTS

The appellants/plaintiffs in this appeal who are pharmaceutical companies, duly registered by the Corporate Affairs Commission (CAC), were at various times between 1st November, 2005 and 26th January, 2006 served Demand Notices by the respondent/defendant for the payment of Business Premises Permit under the Abuja Municipal Area Council Bye-Law, Vol. 1, Cap. 7. The respondent/defendant on several occasions was alleged to have used thugs and members of the Nigerian Police Force to coerce the appellants/plaintiffs to pay the levy imposed in the name of the Business Premises Permit. Also alleged is that on several occasions, the superintendent pharmacists of some of the appellants/plaintiffs were unlawfully arrested and detained and in the process, their premises were closed down.

Aggrieved by the imposition of the levy and other acts of intimidation alleged against the respondent/defendant, the appellants as plaintiffs initiated this action at the

Federal High Court, Abuja, after serving pre-action notice on the respondent/defendant.

The claims of the appellants/plaintiffs at the trial court and contained on pages 3 and 4 of the records are as follows:

1. A DECLARATION that the imposition of the tax or levy whatsoever called (Business Premises Permit or Registration Levy or Fees) on the plaintiffs by the defendant is illegal.
2. A DECLARATION that the provisions of the defendants Bye-Law (Abuja Municipal Area Council Bye-Laws, Vol. 1, Cap. 7f 2001) or whatsoever called seeking to license or register the plaintiff are inconsistent with the constitution and, therefore, void or inoperative.
3. A DECLARATION that the Pharmacists Council of Nigeria is the only competent authority to license or register pharmaceutical companies in Nigeria.
4. An ORDER of the honourable court compelling the defendant to refund all taxes/levies collected from the plaintiffs in respect of the registration.
5. An ORDER of perpetual injunction restraining the defendant either by herself or her servants, agents or privies from further collection of any taxes/levies in respect of registration or licence from the plaintiff and/or from interfering with the smooth operations of pharmaceutical companies in the Abuja Municipal Area Council.

At the trial, the defendant entered a conditional

appearance and when the case came up for the first time on 8th May 2006 at the trial court, the Honourable Justice A. I. Chikere *suo motu* raised the issue of the jurisdiction of the court to try the originating summons and ordered the parties to address the court through written addresses. The trial judge held that the Federal High Court lacked jurisdiction over the suit. The plaintiff/ appellant filed a notice of appeal.

ISSUE FOR DETERMINATION

Whether the Federal High Court was right to decline jurisdiction to hear the suit?

HELD

In whatever way the claims of the plaintiffs/appellants are looked at, they neither fall into matters within the Companies and Allied Matters Act (CAMA) or Companies Income Tax Act, (CITA) or such as can, by any stretch of legislative interpretation, would CAMA be taken or referred to as an agent or agency of the Federal Government in order to smuggle in the process or suit into the Federal High Court. For want of a better language there is no vacancy therein to accommodate such a venture and the trial Federal High Court was right to have hung its decision on *Okoyode v. FCDA* (supra) to arrive at its decision that it lacked the jurisdiction to adjudicate since the Business Premises Levy in issue does not qualify within the ambit of federal callable taxation which would have given that court the jurisdiction needed to proceed.

CUSTOMS AND EXCISE 251(1)(c)

IN THE COURT OF APPEAL OF NIGERIA

CA/E/31/2005

NZUBE ANAZODO v. PAZMECK INTER TRADE, NIGERIA & ANOR

Citation: (2008) 6 NWLR (Pt. 1084) Page 529

Date: On Thursday, the 14th day of June, 2007

FACTS

The plaintiffs, now respondents, sued the defendant now appellant for the sum of five million naira being special and general damages caused to the plaintiffs by the wrongful act of the defendant at the Nnewi High Court in Anambra State of Nigeria.

ISSUE FOR DETERMINATION

Whether the holding by the learned trial judge that the State High Court has jurisdiction to entertain this suit in spite of the issues pertaining to the revenue of the Government of the Federation and operations of Nigerian Customs Service inextricably interwoven in the subject matter of the appeal was correct in view of the provisions of section 251 of the 1999 Constitution of Nigeria?

HELD

A perusal of the said section 251(1)(a) and (c) of the constitution quoted above envisages a civil case or matter relating to the revenue of the government of the Federation in which the said government or an organ thereat or a person suing or being sued on behalf of the Federal Government is a party. In the instant case, neither the Federal Government nor any of its organs or agencies was a party to the suit in the lower court. The case of the respondents/cross appellants was based on losses suffered by them as a result of wrong doing on the part of the appellant; and mere reference to the board of Customs is not the same as a claim by or against the Nigerian Customs Service per **Bada, JCA.**

BANKING S. 251(1)(d)

In the Supreme Court of Nigeria

Suit No: SC.92/2003

NIGERIA DEPOSIT INSURANCE CORPORATION (LIQUIDATOR OF ALLIED BANK OF NIGERIA PLC) v. OKEM ENTERPRISES LIMITED & ANOR.

Citation: (2004) 10 NWLR (Pt. 880) 107

Date: On Friday, the 23rd day of April, 2004

FACTS

The licence of Allied Bank of Nigeria Plc (the bank) was revoked by the Central Bank of Nigeria and this led to the NDIC being appointed the liquidator of the bank. At the date of the revocation of the said licence, The 1st respondent, Okem Enterprises Nigeria Limited, was indebted to the bank in the sum of N284,109,459.59. The NDIC filed an application for the recovery of debt in the Failed Banks (Recovery of Debts) and Financial Malpractices in Banks Tribunal (the tribunal) Lagos Zone, on 29th March, 1999 against the 1st respondent and the 2nd–6th respondents who, at all times material to the action, were the directors of the 1st respondent. This was done by virtue of the Failed Banks (Recovery of Debts) and Financial Malpractices in Banks Decree No. 18 of 1994. That decree was amended by Decree No. 62

of 1999, substituting the Federal High Court for the tribunal. This suit was accordingly taken over by the Federal High Court, Lagos after the inception of the present democratic dispensation, trial by tribunal having been discontinued.

On 16th April, 2000, the respondents filed a notice of objection to the jurisdiction of the Federal High Court to entertain the suit, and sought to have the suit struck out. There were four grounds relied on for the objection, namely, that:

1. The proviso to section 251(1)(d) of the 1999 Constitution of the Federal Republic of Nigeria, repeats the terms of section 230(1)(d) of the 1979 Constitution (as amended by Decree 107 of 1993) and did not vest in the Federal High Court the jurisdiction to determine cases and matters relating to transactions between an individual customer and his bank.
2. The reliefs sought in this suit are matters within the exclusive jurisdiction of the State High Court, etc.

In a short but well considered ruling, given on 18th December, 2000, Abutu J. came to the conclusion that in cases and matters between a bank and its individual customer, the Federal High Court and the State High Courts have concurrent jurisdiction. The learned trial judge overruled the objection.

An appeal was lodged by the defendants against that decision to the Court of Appeal, Lagos Division. The Court of Appeal on 4th February, 2003, allowed the appeal. It held that the Federal High Court has no jurisdiction to entertain cases and matters about individual customer and bank relationship.

NDIC appealed against that decision to the Supreme Court. The appeal was allowed.

ISSUE FOR DETERMINATION

"Whether the Court of Appeal was right in its interpretation of the proviso to section 251(1)(d) of the 1999 Constitution and the effect given to Decree No. 18 of 1994, as amended by Decree No. 62 of 1999, in reaching the conclusion that the State High Courts have exclusive jurisdiction in disputes between an individual customer and his bank?"

HELD

1. "Plainly, the proviso in question, in section 251(1)(d), to put it in simple analysis, says that the Federal High Court will have exclusive jurisdiction in banking matters but when what is involved is an individual customer and his bank transaction, the Federal High Court shall not have exclusive jurisdiction. Understandably, that was to recognise the jurisdiction the State High Courts had been exercising in such matters, which section 272(1) of the constitution impliedly preserves. The High Court of a state can only exercise jurisdiction in any aspect of such specified matters to the extent that the proviso in section 251(1)(d) permits. The said

proviso cannot be interpreted to have the effect of conferring exclusive jurisdiction on the State High Courts and completely taking away the jurisdiction of the Federal High Court to entertain cases and matters relating to individual customers and bank transactions as was erroneously decided by the court below and unsuccessfully argued before this court", per **Uwaifo, JSC** at p. 183, para. E-H

2. "Therefore, the proper view of the proviso in section 251(1)(d) of the 1999 Constitution is that the main provision having used the language of exclusive jurisdiction, the proviso then relaxes that exclusiveness given to the Federal High Court therein, in a situation in which the issue is a dispute between an individual customer and his bank in respect of transactions between the individual and the bank. In that regard, a State High Court will also have or continue to exercise jurisdiction and this it does concurrently with the Federal High Court. There should be no difficulty in appreciating this" per **Uwaifo, JSC** at pp. 185-186, para. H-C

3. "There is no rational basis, as has been shown, for holding that under section 251(1)(d) of the 1999 Constitution, State High Courts have exclusive jurisdiction to determine disputes between an individual customer and his bank in respect of transactions between the individual customer and the bank. It has been demonstrated that in such matters the Federal High Court and State High

Courts have concurrent jurisdiction", per **Uwaifo, JSC** at p. 188, para. A-B

4. "The question which easily comes to mind is: Does the proviso exclude the Federal High Court from exercising jurisdiction in the area contained therein? Or is the Federal High Court simply not allowed to exercise exclusive jurisdiction in the area, and in which case it shares that jurisdiction concurrently with other courts, in this case the State High Courts?

The proviso to my mind is intended not to deny the Federal High Court of jurisdiction in the matter or area stated therein. The proviso is an exception to the "exclusively," rule embodied in section 251(1)(d). In other words, it is a proviso to the provision of paragraph (d) of section 251 subsection (1) only.

Now, it should be appreciated that the words or provision "any dispute between an individual customer and his bank in respect of transactions between individual customer and the bank", per **Kutigi, JSC.** at p. 191, para. F-H

In the Supreme Court of Nigeria

S.C. 342/2001

INTEGRATED TIMBER AND PLYWOOD PRODUCTS LIMITED v. UNION BANK NIGERIA PLC

Citation: (2006) 12 NWLR (Pt. 995) 483

Date: On Friday, the 19th day of May 2006

FACTS

The appellant claimed in the writ of summons taken out on 10th October, 1996, before the Federal High Court, Benin City as follows:

> The defendant which carries on banking business nationwide, has offices in Benin within the jurisdiction of this honourable court.
>
> Sometime in 1990, the defendant while carrying on its banking business forwarded to the plaintiff and irrevocable documentary letter of credit, No. K16167/ 65626 established in Belgium and by a letter dated 12th October, 1990, the defendant advised and confirmed the authenticity of the letter of credit. Pursuant to the defendant's advice and confirmation, the plaintiff adopted the letter of credit and exported Iroko furniture component's worth M28527 to one C.J.E. Dubois Stockmanivs in Belgium. In spite of repeated demand (sic), the plaintiff has received no payment for its goods.

> Wherefore the plaintiff's claims against the defendant the sum of N120,000,000. 00 (one hundred and twenty million naira) as special and general damages for breach of contract and or negligent mis-statement.

The respondent upon being served with the statement of claim, filed a motion on notice on 24th March, 1997, praying for,

> An order dismissing and/or striking out the suit on the grounds (sic) that the court lacks jurisdiction to entertain the suit.

The learned trial judge, Abutu J. of the Federal High Court Benin City, after hearing arguments from both learned counsel for the parties, in a considered ruling delivered on 7th July, 1997, dismissed the said motion, holding that the Federal High Court had jurisdiction to entertain the suit.

Dissatisfied, the respondent successfully appealed to the Court of Appeal (hereinafter called "the court below") which on 12th July, 2000, unanimously allowed the appeal. The appellant being aggrieved by the said decision has now appealed to the Supreme Court on two (2) grounds of appeal. Without their particulars, they read as follows:

1. The learned justices having rightly referred to the claim and statement of claim erred in law in holding:

> Taking into consideration the two definitions above, it cannot be disputed that the dispute that gave rise to this action falls within the confines of the relationship between a bank and customer in which case, the

jurisdiction of the Federal High Court has been ousted by the proviso to paragraph (d) of section 230 (1) of the 1979 Constitution as amended by Decree 107 of 1993.

2. The learned justices erred in law when they held:

   With the greatest respect to the learned trial judge, I disagree with him, that section 1(1) (h) of the Admiralty Jurisdiction of Decree No. 59 of 1991 has conferred jurisdiction on the trial court when the said section ceases to have effect by virtue of the modification of the constitution by Decree No. 107 of 1993. See *Bi Zee Bee Hotels Limited v. Allied Bank (Nigeria) Limited* (1996) 2 NWLR (Pt. 465) 376......

ISSUE FOR DETERMINATION

Whether the learned justices were right in holding that the Federal High Court lacked the jurisdiction to entertain the claim of the plaintiff?

HELD

1. "The transaction between the appellant and the respondent, I hold, was not even that of a banker and customer as was erroneously, with respect, held by the court below. What the appellant has stated from the averments, in my respectful view, was the confirmation of the authenticity of the telex establishing the letter of credit and not the letter of credit itself. Period! The payment of N25.00 (twenty-five naira),was for the said confirmation or in other

words, the consideration paid by the appellant for the said confirmation. I repeat, there was no other transaction of issuance of a letter of credit, between the appellant and the respondent.

Fifthly and lastly, the said confirmation for the consideration or payment of N25.00 (twenty-five naira) amount in my humble but firm views, to a simple contract", per **Ogbuagu, JSC** at 501-502, para. G-A

2. "It is now firmly established, that in a simple contract (as in the instant case between the parties), it is the High Court and not the Federal High Court that has jurisdiction to entertain and determine it. See the case of *Omosowan & 2 Ors v. Chiedozie* (1998) 9 NWLR (Pt. 566) 477 @ 484 C.A.

   I therefore, hold that the court below was right, when it held that, the Federal High Court, lacked jurisdiction to entertain the appellant's suit and consequently, transferred it to the Delta State High Court for hearing and determination", per **Ogbuagu, JSC** at p. 504, para. C-E

IN THE SUPREME COURT OF NIGERIA

On Friday, the 2nd day of May, 2003

Suit No: SC.186/2000

TRADE BANK PLC v. BENILUX (NIG.) LTD

Citation: (2003) 9 NWLR (Part 825) pg. 416

FACTS

Benilux (Nigeria) Limited, who hereinafter shall be referred to as the respondent, herein was the plaintiff at the Lagos State High Court. The respondent had business transaction with Messrs Accountable Finance and Investment Company. As a result of the business transaction Messrs Accountable Finance and Investment Company Limited, issued cheque No. 03370-031150013 A/C No. 102-3720151-01-95, dated 27th January, 1993, in the sum of N1,000,000.00 (one million naira) payable to the respondent. The cheque was marked "A/C Payee only" and "Not Negotiable". It was to be drawn on the account of the company at Martins Street Branch of Trade Bank Plc. Trade Bank Plc is the appellant, in this appeal. In the cheque the appellant was mandated to pay the sum of N1,000,000.00 to the respondent. Instead of paying the amount to the respondent the appellant paid the one million naira to a stranger.

The respondent instituted an action at the State High Court seeking redress against the appellant.

The appellant by way of motion on notice, dated 14th December, 1994, prayed for striking out the suit for lack of jurisdiction of the trial court. In a considered ruling, the trial High Court judge held that the State High Court had jurisdiction to hear the suit. The appeal filed by the appellant was dismissed. It is against the said judgment that the appellant has filed this appeal.

ISSUE FOR DETERMINATION

Whether the High Court of Lagos State is vested with jurisdiction to hear and determine the plaintiff's claim?

HELD

I have no doubt that the respondent, in the case in hand; can sue the appellant, in conversion, for the proceeds of the cheque which the appellant paid to a stranger who is not the payee of the cheque. The plaintiff/respondent's case is simply a tort of conversion and the action filed by the plaintiff/respondent against the appellant can be entertained by any State High Court, per **Mohammed, JSC** at pp. 431-432, para. H-A

In the Supreme Court of Nigeria

Suit No SC.66/1997

FEDERAL MORTGAGE BANK OF NIGERIA v. NIGERIA DEPOSIT INSURANCE CORPORATION (Liquidator of United Commercial Bank Limited)

Citation: (1999) 2 NWLR (Pt. 591) 333

Date: On Friday, the 12th day of February, 1999

FACTS

The appellant placed the sum of N5,000,000.00 (five million naira) on a short-term deposit with the United Commercial Bank on 08/12/92 at an interest of 40% per annum. There were rollovers and the deposit eventually matured on 6th March, 1994. The United Commercial Bank defaulted in paying back the said deposit and interest and the appellant sued the bank claiming as follows:

(a) The sum of N5,000,000.00 (five million naira) being the principal amount paid on the short-term deposit/ placement made on the effective date of 8th December, 1992 by the plaintiff with and in favour of the defendant and which the said sum finally matured on 6th March, 1994 after four rollovers which the defendant had refused and failed to repay despite demands by the plaintiff;

(b) Interest on the above mentioned sum at the agreed

rate of 40% per annum from 6th December, 1993 to 6th March, 1994, being the effective and maturity dates respectively on the 4th rollover;

(c) Interest on the said sum, at an agreed rate of 40% per annum from 6th March, 1994 (being the agreed maturity date of the 4th rollover) until judgment is given and thereafter at the rate of 15% per annum until full repayment.

The United Commercial Bank did not enter appearance or file any defence. Judgment was therefore entered in favour of the appellant on 12th July, 1994. The United Commercial Bank did not appeal against the judgment. The appellant took steps and levied execution and attached the goods and chattels of the United Commercial Bank on 5th September, 1994. The goods and chattels were attached down within the judgment-debtor's premises by the deputy sheriff. On 9th September, 1994, the Central Bank of Nigeria revoked the banking license of United Commercial Bank and appointed the respondent herein to liquidate the bank. Acting on the appointment, the respondent proceeded to remove the goods and chattels of the United Commercial Bank which had been attached and put same in its possession and control which act prevented the deputy sheriff from going ahead to effect a sale of same to realize the judgment. As a result of this development, the appellant on 15th September, 1994 applied to the High Court by motion, praying the court to compel the respondent to produce the attached goods and chattels of United Commercial Bank and to direct the deputy sheriff to effect sale of same. This motion was argued on 23th September, 1994 and ruling was reserved to 14th October, 1994. On 5th October, 1994, the respondent herein applied by motion on notice to the court for an order to arrest the ruling fixed for 14th October, 1994 and to stay proceedings pending the outcome of the appeal upon the ground that the High Court had no jurisdiction to adjudicate on the matter.

The application was predicated on an appeal filed by the respondent on 4th October, 1994 against the judgment of 12th July, 1994.

However, that appeal was not pursued by the respondent. The respondent's motion was argued on 14th October, 1994 and dismissed. Thereupon, the High Court delivered its ruling on the appellant's motion of 15th October, 1994 and granted the prayers sought therein. Dissatisfied, the respondent appealed against the ruling to the Court of Appeal. The Court of Appeal, sitting as a full court, allowed the respondent's appeal. It set aside the judgment of 12th July, 1994 and the ruling of 14th October, 1994 on the ground that the High Court had no jurisdiction. The appellant was dissatisfied and appealed to the Supreme Court. The respondent was also dissatisfied with some parts of the judgment and it cross-appealed. The Supreme Court unanimously dismissed the appeal and the cross appeal.

ISSUES FOR DETERMINATION

1. Is the appellant a 'bank' within the contemplation

of section 230(1)(d) of the constitution (Suspension and Modification) Decree No. 107 of 1993?

2. Does Lagos State High Court share a concurrent jurisdiction with the Federal High Court in respect of banker-customer disputes/transactions as provided in the proviso to section 230(1)(d) of Decree No. 107 of 1993, etc?

HELD

On the Definition of the Word "Bank"

1. 'The word "bank" is not defined in the constitution or in the Interpretation Act. However, in its ordinary grammatical meaning, it means an organisation or place that provides financial service", per **M.E. Ogundare, JSC** at 361 para. B.

On the Status of the Federal Mortgage Bank as a Bank

2. "Having regard to the provisions of the law setting it up, particularly sections 5(1)(a) and 6(1)(a) & (b) of the Federal Mortgage Bank Decree No. 82 of 1993,I think it is right to say that it(the Federal Mortgage Bank) falls within this ordinary meaning", per **M. E. Ogundare, JSC** at 361, para. C-E.

On which Court Is Competent to Try Action between One Bank and Another over a Debt

3. I do not share the view that the proviso in section 230(1)(d) (now section 251(1)(d) of the 1999

Constitution) would apply where in a customer/ banker relationship, the customer is a bank. To say that where there is a dispute between two banks, the forum for the resolution of the dispute is the Federal High Court to read into section 230(1)(d) now S. 251(1)(d) of the 1999 Constitution what is not there. A lot depends on the nature of the transaction.... I must hold that it is a simple customer/banker relationship which the proviso in section 230(1)(d) exempts from the exclusive jurisdiction of the Federal High Court," per **Ogundare, JSC** at 362, para. H–363 para. A.

Operation of CAMA S. 251 (1)(e)

In the Supreme Court of Nigeria

Suit No: SC.237/2005

ADETONA and 2 ORS v. IGELE GENERAL ENTERPRISES LIMITED

Citation: (2011) 7 NWLR (Pt. 1247) 535

Date: On Friday, the 14th day of January, 2011

FACTS

Sometime in June, 2000, the 1st appellant took over the management of the 2nd appellant following his appointment as receiver/manager of the 2nd appellant by the 3rd appellant. On 7th December, 2000 (six months after the takeover), the 1st appellant in the purported exercise of his duties broke into and locked up the premises at 27A Fatai Atere Way, Matori Mushin, Lagos, which premises also housed the respondents' office and warehouse. The respondent is an independent business concern which happens to share the same premises with the 2nd appellant. The respondent brought an action before the Lagos High Court against the appellant challenging the act of the 1st appellant because the 1st appellant refused it access to its office and warehouse in which its chemicals and other properties worth millions of naira were kept until 6th April, 2001, in spite of efforts by the respondent to convince him to open up the premises.

The appellant filed a notice of preliminary objection, dated 16th October, 2001, challenging the jurisdiction of the trial court to hear and determine the suit on the ground that the Federal High Court is the court vested with jurisdiction in respect of the subject matter of the suit. Oshodi (J), dismissed the objection and held that the court has jurisdiction to entertain the suit.

Aggrieved with the above ruling, the appellants appealed against same to the Lagos division of the Court of Appeal. The lower court in its judgment on 10th March, 2005, dismissed the appeal and upheld the decision of the trial court, assuming jurisdiction to entertain action instituted by the respondent.

This is an appeal against the decision of the Court of Appeal, Lagos division delivered on 10th March, 2005 whereby, the court dismissed the appeal lodged by the appellant against the ruling of the High Court of Lagos state, which dismissed the appellants' preliminary objection dated 16th October, 2010 in which they sought to strike out the respondent's suit on the ground that the suit arose from the exercise of powers and duties of a receiver/manager and therefore falls within the operations of the Companies and Allied Matters Act, over which the Federal High Court has exclusive jurisdiction by virtue of the provision of section 251(1)(e) of the 1999 Constitution of the Federal Republic of Nigeria.

ISSUE FOR DETERMINATION

"Whether, from the respondent's claim and the circumstances of this case, the Court of Appeal was right in holding that the High Court of Lagos state has jurisdiction to entertain the respondent's suit?"

HELD

On the Jurisdiction of the Federal High Court to Determine Civil Cases and Arising from the Operations of the Companies and Allied Matters Act

1. "The Federal High Court has, to the exclusion of any other court, jurisdiction to hear and determine civil cases and matters arising from the operations of the Companies and Allied Matters Act or any other enactment regulating the operation of the companies and Allied Matters Act or any enactment regulating the operation of companies incorporated under the Act," per **Suleiman Galadima, JSC** p 558, para. C–D.

Jurisdiction of the Trial Court where the Operation of the Companies and Allied Matters Act is not Directly in Issue

2. "Quite clearly a careful study of the above averments in the statement of claim and the writ of summons reveal that it is not a matter arising from the operation of the Companies and Allied Matters Act Cap 20 Laws of the Federation of Nigeria 2004, but

the claim was based on an action that arose as a result of the relationship of the 2nd appellant and his landlord. The court below is therefore right to affirm that the High Court of Lagos State had jurisdiction to heal the case," per **A. M. Mukhtar, JSC** p. 562, para. D–F.

IN THE SUPREME COURT OF NIGERIA

Suit No: SC.88/2005

ABIOLA & SONS BOTTLING COMPANY NIGERIA LIMITED & Anor v. FIRST CITY MERCHANT BANK LIMITED

Citation:

(2013) LPELR-20387(SC)

(2013) 4 MJSC. 122

Date: On Friday, the 19th day of April, 2013

FACTS

By a deed of debenture, dated 27th November, 1986, between the plaintiffs and the 1st defendant, the sum of N3,500,000 (three million, five hundred thousand naira) was advanced in the form of a term loan overdraft facilities to the 1st plaintiffs to meet their working capital requirement and finances to import raw materials. As the plaintiffs defaulted in repaying the loan, the 1st defendant exercised its powers under clause 11 of the Deed of debenture and appointed the 2nd defendant as a receiver/manager. In the exercise of his powers as such, the 2nd defendant sold off some of the 1st plaintiffs' assets to the 3rd defendants. Not happy with the sale, the plaintiffs took out a writ of summons on 1st July, 1991, claiming in paragraph 35 of their joint further amended statement of claim to the following effects:

1. The first declaration sought, attacks the Debenture

Deed made between the respondents and the 1st appellant. (Part VII of the Companies and Allied Matters Act, that is, sections 166-210, deals with all matters pertaining to debentures including the remedies prescribed for debenture holder which is the appointment of a receiver).

2. Second and third reliefs relate to the appointment of the 2nd appellant as a receiver pursuant to the said Debenture Deed. (The powers, duties and liabilities etc. of a receiver or receiver/manager are governed by section 387 of the Act.)
3. The fourth and fifth reliefs attack the power of the receiver to sell off the plaintiffs' assets or properties.
4. The sixth relief complains about the 2nd appellant's failure to account to the Registrar of Companies which is covered by section 393 of the Act.
5. The twelfth, thirteenth and sixteenth reliefs ask for an account from the 2nd appellant. (This relates to section 396 of the Act.)

The suit was commenced at the Kwara State High Court on 1st July, 1991 and was pending when Decree No. 107 (Constitution [suspension modification] Decree of 1993 was enacted. The said decree amended S. 230 (1) of the 1979) constitution. The amended provision is *impari material* with S. 251(1) of the 1999 Constitution which itemised the exclusive jurisdiction of the Federal High Court.

The defendants at the trial court filed a preliminary objection challenging the jurisdiction of the State High

Court to try the suit as it was predicated on the operation of the Companies and Allied Matters Act. The objection was dismissed by the trial court. The Court of Appeal allowed the appeal against the decision of the trial State High Court. The plaintiff appealed to the Supreme Court.

ISSUE FOR DETERMINATION

Whether having regard to the circumstances of this case, the learned justices of the Court of Appeal erred in law when they held that the trial State High Court had/has no requisite jurisdiction to hear and determine the plaintiffs (now appellants) suit/claims?

HELD

On the Jurisdiction of the Federal High Court over the Operation of the Companies And Allied Matters Act

1. "Most of the respondents' claims fell squarely within the armpit of the provisions made by Decree 107 of 1993, section 230(1) thereof as they are cases and matters arising from the operation of an act or Decree relating to Companies and Allied Matters. Afortiori, it is the Federal High Court that can competently exercise jurisdiction on such matters and I so hold", per **Muhammad, JSC**.

IN THE COURT OF APPEAL OF NIGERIA

CA/B/265/2009

CHIEF KENNETH GBAGI & ANOR v. CHIEF T. J. ONOMIGBO OKPOKO

Citation: (2014) 4 NWLR (Pt. 1396) Page 136

Date: On Friday, the 15th day of February, 2013

FACTS

The respondent, as plaintiff in the lower court, filed an action against the appellants (as defendants) seeking, in the main:

> an order of specific performance that the defendants do transfer to the plaintiff all the shares held in their names in the books of NEM Insurance Plc as at 23rd November, 2000 upon the plaintiff depositing with the Registrar of this honourable court, a bank draft drawn in favour of either the 1st or 2nd defendant in the sum of N4,437,984.00.

The respondent sought other reliefs in the alternative. The writ of summons and statement of claim showing those reliefs are contained on pages 1 to 6 of the Record of Appeal. The appellants entered conditional appearance as shown on page 22 of the Record of Appeal and filed a Notice of Preliminary Objection dated and filed 10th December, 2007 as shown on pages 23 to 26 of the Record of Appeal, querying *inter alia*, the jurisdiction of the court to entertain the suit on account of the fact that the subject matter of the suit has to do with the transfer of shares of a company registered under the Companies and Allied Matter Act which the company was not even a party to the suit. The respondent (plaintiff) responded by filing an application for default judgment dated 11th January, 2008.

In the meantime, unknown to the appellants, the said Notice of Preliminary Objection had been of struck out on 10th January, 2008 when the matter came up. As far as the appellants (defendants) could tell, there was no hearing notice on them for the hearing of that Notice of Preliminary Objection. The lower court heard the application of the respondent for default judgment and granted same on 26th February, 2008. The appellants filed a number of applications to set aside the default judgment which applications were not moved and struck out. In the meantime, the matter was transferred from Warri Judicial division where the application dated 17th November, 2008 to set aside the default judgment of 26th February, 2008 was finally heard and determined by Ohwo J. who refused the said application.

ISSUE FOR DETERMINATION

Whether it is the Federal or State High Court that has jurisdiction in the instant matter?

HELD

1. The jurisdiction of the Federal High Court under the 1999 Constitution of the Federal Republic of Nigeria is

to be found as correctly cited by the learned counsel to the respondent under section 251, and not section 250 as erroneously cited by Counsel to the appellants.

Section 251(1)(e) of the 1999 Constitution provides as follows:

Section 251(1)

> Notwithstanding anything to the contrary contained in this Constitution and in addition to such other jurisdiction as may be conferred upon it by an Act of the National Assembly, the Federal High Court shall have and exercise jurisdiction to the exclusion of any other Court in civil cases and matters:
>
> **(e)** arising from the operation of the Companies and Allied Matters Act or any other enactment replacing that Act or regulating the operation of Companies incorporated under the Companies and Allied Matters Act.

The provisions of section 251(1)(e) of the 1999 Constitution of Federal Republic of Nigeria, the interpretation thereto is already settled by the Supreme Court of Nigeria in the case of *Tanarewa (Nig.) Limited v. Plastic Fair Limited (supra)* cited and solely relied upon by the learned counsel to the appellants. Under the Doctrine of *Stare Decisis,* all other courts including this court are bound to follow and make the similar interpretation to those provisions. The Supreme Court at pp. 375-376, para. B-C on the extent and scope of jurisdiction of the Federal High Court in relation to matters arising from the operations of the Companies and Allied Matters Act stated as follows:

> By virtue of section 251(1)(e) of the 1999 Constitution, notwithstanding anything to the contrary contained in the Constitution and in addition to such other jurisdiction as may be conferred upon it by an Act of the National Assembly, the Federal High Court shall have and exercise jurisdiction to the exclusion of any other court in civil cases and matters arising from the operation of the Companies and Allied Matters Act or any other enactment replacing that Act or regulating operation of companies incorporated under the companies and Allied Matters Act.
>
> It is manifest from the foregoing provisions that jurisdiction will only vest in the Federal High Court if the suit involves civil cases and matters arising from the operation of the Companies and Allied Matters Act or any other Act replacing that Act or regulating the operation of companies incorporated under the Companies and Allied Matters Act. The implication is that in an action involving regulating, running or management or control of companies, the Federal High Court would be vested with jurisdiction.
>
> Thus, an action could be maintained and entertained in matters affecting formation or winding-up of a company; memorandum and articles of association; shares and shareholding; appointment, removal or change or alteration of directors. It also

includes appointment of receiver and his various obligations such as giving notice of his appointment, filing statement of accounts with the Corporate Affairs Commission as contained in various provisions of CAMA, particularly sections 393, 996, 398 and 399. These provisions control the conduct of a receiver and any claim arising from the breach thereof or enforcing right thereunder will qualify as an action arising from the operation of the said Act or regulation. But where the dispute does not involve the control or administration of a company and deals with ordinary routine business of a company, a State High court, and not the Federal High Court, has jurisdiction to entertain and determine the matter," per **Sidi Bage, JCA** at pages 152-3, para. B-G.

2. That is to say, any matter that can be decided without recourse to either the Companies and Allied Matters Act, or any enactment regulating operation of companies under the said Act belongs to a State High Court, *University of Ilorin Teaching Hospital v. Akilo* (2001) 4 NWLR (pt. 703) 246; *F.M.B.N. v. NDIC* (1999) 2 NWLR (pt. 591) 333; *Ali v. CBN* (1997) 4 NWLR (pt. 498) 192; *University of Abuja v. Ologe* (1996) 4 NWLR (pt. 445) 706; *NIDB v. Fembo Nig. Limited* (1997) 2 NWLR (pt. 489) 543; *Bi Zee Bee Hotels Limited v. Allied Bank of Nigeria Limited* (1996) 8 NWLR (Pt. 465) 176; 7-up *Bottling Co. Limited v. Abiola & Sons Bottling Co. Limited* (1996) 7 NWLR (pt. 463) 714; *Jammal Steel Structures Limited v. ACB Limited* (1973) 1 ALL NLR (pt.2) 208 referred to," per **Sidi Bage, JCA** at 153-4, para. H-B

3. It is thus clear from the interpretation of the apex court to those provisions, that the jurisdiction of the Federal High Court in civil cases and matters arising from the operation of the Companies and Allied Matters would include actions involving regulating, running or management or control of companies.

   Thus, an action could be maintained and entertained by the Federal High Court affecting formation or winding down of a company; memorandum and articles of association; shares and shareholding; appointment, removal or change or alteration of directors. It also includes appointment of receiver and his various obligations such as giving notice of his appointment, filing statements of accounts with the Corporate Affairs Commission as contained in various provisions of CAMA, particularly sections 393, 396, 398 and 399.

"These provisions control the conduct of a receiver and any claim arising from a breach thereof or enforcing right thereunder will qualify as action arising from the operation of the said Act or regulation. It is very clear that, the Supreme Court is referring to the operations of a company incorporated under the Companies and Allied Matters Act. The shares and share holding herein refers to the shares and share holding of that company. What if the company in the course of its business goes to acquire the shares of another company, the apex court answered this question immediately in this same case of Tanarewa Nig. Limited, (supra). It stated that, where the dispute does not involve the control or administration of company and deals with ordinary routine business of a company, a State High Court, and not the Federal High Court has jurisdiction to entertain and determine the matter," per **Sidi Bage, JCA** at 154 B-G.

COPYRIGHTS, TRADEMARK S. 251(1)(f)

IN THE SUPREME COURT OF NIGERIA

SC.79/2005

SOCIETY BIC S.A. & ORS v. CHARZIN INDUSTRIES LIMITED

Citation: (2014) 4 NWLR (Pt. 1398) Page 497

Date: On Friday, the 14th day of February, 2014

FACTS

Before the High Court of Justice of Lagos State, Lagos Judicial Division, the plaintiff, now respondent, claimed against the defendants, now appellants, as follows:

(a) The sum of N10,000,000.00 (ten million naira) as damages for injury suffered by reason of the libel on the plaintiff's "CHARZIN" ballpoint pens contained in the advertisements the defendants published and caused to be published in the issues of the *Vanguard Newspaper*, of August 18, 1995 on Page 10 and the *Daily Times Newspaper* of November 13, 1995 on Page 4.

(b) A perpetual injunction restraining the defendants and each of them whether by themselves or by their servants or agents from further printing, issuing, publishing or circulating or causing to be printed, issued, published or any other similar libel affecting the plaintiff.

The plaintiff filed its statement of claim along with the writ of summons. The reliefs were predicated on the grounds that:

1. By the provisions of section 230(1) subsection (f) of the Constitution (suspension and modification), Decree No. 107 of 1993, (*impari material* with S. 251(1)(f) of the 1999 Constitution) jurisdiction is conferred on the Federal High Court to the exclusion of all other courts, with respect to civil and criminal cases or matters relating to:

> Any Federal enactment relating to copyright, patents, designs, trademarks and passing-off, industrial designs and merchandise marks, business names and commercial industrial monopolies, combines and torts, standards of goods and commodities and industrial standards.

2. The claim in this suit arising from a publication made on protection of the defendants' registered trademarks, copyrights and design falls within the exclusive jurisdiction of the Federal High Court as provided for under the constitution (Suspension and Modification) Decree No. 107 of 1993.

Upon service on them of the writ and statement of claim, the defendants (now appellants) filed a motion on notice on 23rd February, 1998 asking for the following relief *inter alia*:

> An order striking out this suit in that this honourable court has no jurisdiction to entertain the same being an action within the exclusive jurisdiction of the

Federal High Court.

The preliminary objection was dismissed. In a challenge to the ruling on their motion on notice, the defendants/ appellants appealed to the Court of Appeal and lost. A further appeal was lodged before the Supreme Court.

ISSUE FOR DETERMINATION

Whether on the totality of the materials before the Court of Appeal the learned trial judge was right in finding that the cause of action in the suit was founded in the tort of trade libel and not in trademark and therefore the High Court of Lagos State has jurisdiction to hear and determine the respondent's suit?

HELD

Trade Libel Does not Constitute Infringement of trademark

1. The statement of claim reveals that the appellants and the respondents are in the business of manufacturing ballpoint pens. The appellants brand is BIC ballpoint pen, while the respondents' CHARZIN ballpoint pen.

   The publication in the newspapers warns the reading public to avoid the respondents' brand of ballpoint pens as the said products are imitations. The respondent says this is a false and malicious publication by the appellants. This is clearly the tort of libel. Nowhere in the pleadings is an infringing of the respondents trademark remotely alleged. The provisions of section 230(1)(f) of Decree No.107 of 1993 or section 251(1)(f) of the 1999 Constitution are in the circumstances not applicable. The respondents' claim is founded in the Tort of Libel. To be precise, defamation, and injunction to stop further publishing of defamatory material," per, **Bode Rhodes-Vivour, JSC** at 539-540, para. H-B.

On Jurisdiction of the State High Court to Hear a Case of Libel

2. "What was in issue was the false publication to the reading public to avoid imitation. The publication refers to CHARZIN ball point pens as an imitation. The averments in the statement of claim do not complain about trademark infringement of the mark CHARZIN, rather it complains of the false and malicious publication warning the reading public to avoid CHARZIN which is an imitation. That is the effect of "avoid imitation". This is clearly a cause of action that falls into the tort of libel and not copyright or trademark as spelt out by the provisions of section 230(1)(f) of Decree No.107 of 1993 or section 251(1)(f) of the Constitution. Since the claims are for libel and injunction, the State High Court and not the Federal High Court has jurisdiction to hear the plaintiff/respondent claims. Both courts below were correct," per **Bode Rhodes-Vivour, JSC** at page 541, para. E-G.

IN THE SUPREME COURT OF NIGERIA

SC.116/1999

AYMAN ENTERPRISES LIMITED v. AKUMA INDUSTRIES LIMITED & ORS

Citation: [2003] 13 NWLR (pt. 836)22

Date: On Friday, the 20th day of June, 2003

FACTS

This action originated from the Federal High Court Lagos. The main claim was for passing off against the plaintiff's trademark. The trial court granted an *anton pillar* order, ex parte, against the defendant which was successfully challenged and set aside at the Court of Appeal. The appellant then appealed to the Supreme Court from the decision of the Court of Appeal and the respondents also cross-appealed.

ISSUE FOR DETERMINATION

Whether the Federal High Court has jurisdiction to entertain a claim for damages for "passing-off' of an unregistered trademark.

HELD

Jurisdiction of the Federal High Court in Matters Involving Trademarks and Passing-off

1. The jurisdiction of the Federal High Court at the

material time, is as set out in section 230(1)(f) of the 1979 Constitution, as amended, by Decree No. 107 of the 1993 and section 7 of the Federal High Court Act, 1973 (Cap. 134 Laws of the Federation of Nigeria, 1990), section 230(1)(f) of the 1979 Constitution provides:

> Notwithstanding anything to the contrary contained in this Constitution and in addition to such other jurisdiction as may be conferred upon it by an Act of the National Assembly or a Decree, the Federal High Court shall have and exercise jurisdiction *to the exclusion of any other court in civil cases and matters arising from*:
>
> (f) any *Federal enactment relating to* copyright, patents, designs, *trademarks and passing-off*, industrial designs and merchandise marks, business names, and commercial industrial monopolies, combines and trusts, standards of goods and commodities and industrial standards.

By this provision, the Federal High Court and that court alone, had exclusive jurisdiction to entertain all civil cases and matters arising from Federal enactment relating to any of the matters mentioned in (f) above, including trademarks and passing-off," per **U. A. Kalgo, JSC** at 44 -45, para. F-B.

On the Jurisdiction of the Federal High Court in Respect of Unregistered Trademark

2. "The total effect of the judgment in Patkun's case is

that the Federal High Court will only have jurisdiction to entertain an action for passing-off arising from an infringement of a registered trade mark and the action must have arisen in relation to a federal enactment. The Trademark Act, 1965, is a federal enactment, but in this case although there was an allegation of infringement of a trademark, the trademark was not registered and so the passing-off claim, even if there was such passing-off, did not and could not have arisen from a registered trade-mark. Also, the passing-off right of action in Patkun's case is clearly statutory having arisen from the infringement of the Trademark Act, 1965, a federal enactment. I am bound by the decision in Patkun's case as a decision of this court and I follow it. In the instant case, the passing-off right of action did not arise from the infringement of any federal enactment and so may only be a common law right. Therefore, the Federal High Court would not have any jurisdiction under section 230(1)(f) of the 1979 Constitution or S.7(1)(c)(ii) of the Federal High Court Act, 1973 to entertain the passing-off action instituted by the appellant in the instant case. I hold accordingly. I therefore find that the Court of Appeal was wrong when it said in the leading judgment that "the Federal High Court is eminently competent to adjudicate on the matter," per **U. A. Kalgo, JSC** at page 49-50, para. G-H.

Admiralty and shipping S. 251(1)(g)

In the Supreme Court of Nigeria

SC42/2009

PORTS AND CARGO HANDLINGS SERVICE COMPANY LIMITED & ORS v. MIGFO NIGERIA LIMITED & ANOR.

Citation: (2012) 18 NWLR (Pt. 1333) 555

Date: On Friday, the 8th Day of June 2012

FACTS

The plaintiffs' (now the respondents) filed an originating summons before the Federal High Court Lagos over the joint venture agreement between the 2nd appellants and the respondents as to their joint bid for the concession and subsequent operation and management and of Terminal 'C', Tin Can Island Port, Apapa, including the following reliefs:

1. "A declaration that the intentions, declarations, understandings, joint venture agreement and irrevocable commitments expressed by the plaintiffs and the 2nd defendant and contained in the Technical Proposal / Bid documents dated June, 2005 and their executed Memorandum of Understanding dated 27th July, 2005, submitted to the Bureau of Public Enterprises in respect of their bidding for the management and operation of Terminal C, Tin Can

Island Port, Apapa, Lagos in the name of the 2nd defendant, are binding on the plaintiffs and the 2nd defendant.

2. A declaration that by virtue of the intentions, declarations, understanding, joint venture agreement and irrevocable commitments expressed by the plaintiffs and the 2nd defendant and contained in the Technical Proposal / Bid documents dated June, 2005 and their executed Memorandum of Understanding dated 27th July, 2005 submitted to the Bureau of Public Enterprises in the name of the 2nd defendant in respect of their bidding for the management and operation of Terminal C, Tin Can Island Port, Apapa, Lagos, the plaintiffs and the 2nd defendant are joint bidders for and joint-venture partners in respect of the management/operation of, the said Terminal C, Tin Can Island Port, Apapa Lagos."

At the trial Federal High Court, the defendants (now Appellants) raised a preliminary objection to the jurisdiction of that court to entertain the respondents' suit. The trial court though held, that the plaintiffs' claim relates to the management and operation of Terminal 'C' Tin Can Island Port, and that the claim falls within the provision of section 251(1)(g) of the 1999 Constitution. The appellants were dissatisfied and appealed to the Court of Appeal. The appeal was dismissed at that court. The appellants further appealed to the Supreme Court.

ISSUE FOR DETERMINATION

Considering the clear provisions of section 251(1)(g) of the 1999 Constitution which the trial Federal High Court relied upon to assume jurisdiction in this matter, whether or not the lower court was not in grave error to have held as it did, that the Federal High Court rightly assumed jurisdiction in this matter.

HELD

1. On the extent of the jurisdiction of the Federal High Court over admiralty matters and cases related thereto, section 7(3) of the Federal High Court Act reproduced hereunder clearly illustrates this point:

   7. for emphasis (3) where jurisdiction is conferred upon the Court under subsections (1), (2) and (3) of this section, such jurisdiction shall be construed to include jurisdiction to hear and determine all issues relating to, arising from, or ancillary to such subject matter.

From the above, it is clear that the relevant operative phrase is "include jurisdiction to hear and determine all issues relating to, arising from or ancillary to such subject matter." In determining the relevance of the phrase under reference, it is imperative to determine what the sub-phrase "such subject matter" refers to. From the clear provision of the Act, the only natural interpretation of the phrase "such subject matter" are those subject matter(s) identified in subsections (1), (2) and (3) of the Federal High Court Act; which is *impari material* with the provisions of section 251(1)(g) of the Constitution of the

Federal Republic of Nigeria 1999 (as amended).

From the provisions of section 7 (1), (2) and (3) of the Federal High Court, the admiralty cases identified therein has to do with "any admiralty jurisdiction, including shipping and navigation and the Rivers Niger, Benue and their affluent and on such other inland waterway as may be designated by any enactment to be an international waterway, all federal ports, (including the constitution and powers of the ports authorities for Federal ports) and carriage by sea.

The instant suit has nothing to do with shipping and navigation on the Rivers Niger, Benue and their affluent or any inland waterway. It is neither connected with or challenging the constitution and power of the ports authorities for any federal ports, nor does it invoke any dispute arising from a carriage by sea. Considering the provision of section 1(3) of the Admiralty Jurisdiction Act, it is clear that to determine and give effect to its true meaning, the *"expressio unius est exclusio alterius"* maxim of interpretation must be applied. It is a trite rule that where a statute mentions specific things, those things not mentioned are not intended to be included. See *S.E.C v Kasumu* (2001) 10 NWLR (Part 1150) Page 509. Despite the wide admiralty jurisdiction of the Federal High Court, under section 1(1) of the Act, the expression "includes" does not leave the ambit of the court jurisdiction open - ended. It is trite that the jurisdiction of a court cannot be expanded, especially where same has been clearly defined and prescribed by a statute. See *Tukur v Governor of Gongola State* (1989) 4 NWLR (Part 117) Page 517,

Onuorah v K.R.P.C. (supra): *Onwudiwe v F.R.N.* (2006) 10 NWLR (Part 988) Page 382 and *Gafar v Governor of Kwara State* (supra)," per **Galadima, JSC** at 593 para. H-595.

2. Extent of jurisdiction of the Federal High Court in respect of S. 251(1)(g) of the Constitution.

   The admiralty jurisdiction of the Federal High Court is contained in section 251(1)(g) of the 1999 Constitution of the Federal Republic of Nigeria, hereunder reproduced:

   Section 251(1)(g): Any admiralty jurisdiction including shipping and navigation on the River Niger or Benue and their effluents and on such other inland waterway as may be designated by any enactment to be an international waterway, all federal ports (including the constitution and powers of the port, authorities for federal ports) and carriage by sea.

3. The contract entered into by the parties, evidenced by the intention, declarations, understanding, joint venture agreement and irrevocable commitments, the sanctity and enforcement of which contract, the respondent as plaintiff approached the Federal High Court by invoking that court's admiralty jurisdiction is not within the intendment of section 251(1)(g) of the Constitution. It has nothing to do with shipping and/or navigation on any inland waterway or international waterway or federal ports or the constitution and powers of the ports, authorities for federal ports or carriage by sea.

Also, section l (1) of the Admiralty Jurisdiction Act Cap 5 Laws of the Federation 2004, upon which the lower court placed reliance provides:

> (1): The admiralty jurisdiction of the Federal High Court (in the Act referred to as the Court) includes the following:
>
> (g) Any matter, arising within a federal port or a national airport and its precincts, including claims for loss of or damage to goods occurring between off-loading of goods across space from a ship or any aircraft and their delivery at the consignee's premises, or during storage or transportation before delivery to the consignee.
>
> (i) Any case or matter arising from the constitution and powers of all port authorities, airport authority and the National Maritime Authority.

Here again, the dispute between the parties does not fall within the embrace of the provision reproduced above. I do not see how the lower court could have relied on the above provision to affirm the jurisdiction wrongly assumed by the Federal High Court to determine the respondent's case before it.

The jurisdiction of the Federal High Court is wide but it is by no means unlimited and while that court, as any other court, can expound its jurisdiction, it cannot expand it to include any matters over which the law creating it did not vest it with powers to determine," per **Ngwuta, JSC** at page 605, para. E–page 606, para. F.

IN THE SUPREME COURT OF NIGERIA

SC 358/2001

MR. VICTOR ADELEKAN v. ECU-LINE NV

Citation: (2006) 12 NWLR (Pt. 993) 33

Date: On Friday, the 12th day of May 2006

FACTS

Sometime in 1996, the present appellant entered into a contract with the respondent for the carriage by sea of S.T.C. photo processing machine from Canada to Nigeria for valuable consideration. Later on, appellant entered into yet another contract with the respondent, this time for the carriage by sea of a photo plotter MIVA 25 machine from Belgium to Nigeria.

In May 1997, the respondent by fax notified the appellant that the goods have been placed on board the M.V. Kagoro, which was expected to berth in Nigeria on or before 25 May, 1997. Along with the fax message came a copy of the bill of lading No 30504 – MTL - LAG which did not include the photo plotter MIVA 25 machine; the bill of lading only contained the S.T.C. Photo processing machine. The appellant immediately notified the respondent of the omission.

When the ship arrived in Nigeria, the appellant discovered that the photo plotter MIVA 25 machine was not included and the respondent was duly notified and it was later discovered that the photo plotter MIVA 25 machine was misplaced by the respondent in its warehouse.

The respondent admitted liability in letters dated 16th and 30th January, 1998 and offered monetary compensation which the appellant rejected by letters dated 18th January, 1998 and 13th February, 1998 because, according to the appellant, it was below the replacement cost of the machine. By a letter dated 7th October 1998, the appellant's solicitors demanded payment of US $98,520.00 as compensation for the loss but the respondent replied on 19th October 1998 expressing sympathy but contended that the claim was statute barred. The appellant therefore instituted an action in the Federal High Court, Ibadan in suit No FHC/IB/CS/10/99 claiming ₦14,925,639.00 being the money payable by the respondent to the appellant for breach of contract of carriage of goods by sea and negligent loss of goods. The appellant contended in the statement of claim that the photo plotter MIVA 25 machine was misplaced within the respondent's warehouse and that no bill of lading was ever processed for its shipment, that it was never loaded on board the M.V. Kagoro and that the respondent could therefore not avail itself of the defence of limitation of time under the *Hague Visby Rules* for the bringing of an action in respect of carriage of goods by sea.

The main appeal was dismissed on the ground that it was filled out of time and no leave was sought to extend time within which to appeal. The Supreme Court then considered the sole issue in the cross appeal, to wit:

ISSUE FOR DETERMINATION

Whether the lower court, in any event, should not have struck out the cross-respondent's suit on the ground that being a claim for simple contract, the Federal High Court lacked the requisite jurisdiction to entertain the matter?

HELD

"The provisions of section 251 of the Constitution of the Federal Republic of Nigeria, 1999, hereinafter called the 1999 Constitution, are very clear and unambiguous. It is the section that confers jurisdiction on the Federal High Court, which jurisdiction clearly does not include dealing with any case of simple contract or damages for negligence as envisaged by the action before the trial Court.

I therefore have no hesitation in agreeing with learned counsel for the cross appellant that the trial Court had no jurisdiction in the matter as framed before it and ought to have struck same out," per **Onnoghen, JSC** at 52, para. F-H.

In the Court of Appeal of Nigeria

CA/C/122/93

CROWNSTAR & COMPANY LTD v. THE VESSEL MV VALI P. & ORS

Citation: (2000)1NWLR (Pt 639) 37

Date: On Thursday, the 6th day of May, 1999

FACTS

This is an appeal against the decision of Obasse J. of the High Court of Cross River State, holden in Calabar, dated 17th September, 1991. At the High Court of Cross River State, Calabar, the appellant as plaintiff, claimed against the respondents, as defendants, as follows:

(a) By a contract of affreightment evidenced by 3 bills of lading Nos 1,2 and 3 respectively, the 2nd defendant contracted to carry and deliver in good condition from Constanza Seaport, Romania to the plaintiff in Port Harcourt or so near thereto as she may safely get the goods specified therein on board the (2nd defendant's) vessel MV Vali P. 244,000 bags of Romanian Grey Portland Cement of total gross weight of 12,200 metric tons valued at US $915,000.00. On the 15th day of June, 1993, the 3rd defendant MV Vali P. aforesaid notified the plaintiff that the vessel would arrive 5th or 6th July, 1993.

(b) The vessel MV Vali P. however arrived Port Harcourt

on 15th July, 1993, after the plaintiff had booked and cancelled the booking of berths for 5th and 6th of July, 1991 and paid the relevant NPA cancellation of berth charges. On delivery of the cargo to the plaintiff, it was discovered and certified by the plaintiff and the 2nd defendant's agent that 4059 bags or 202.95 metric tons of the cement were in damaged condition, to wit: caked and or wet and or the bags in which they were contained, broken and so damaged as not to retain any salvage value, thereby occasioning great loss to the plaintiff; the damage occurred while cargo was on board the vessel MV Vali P. and before discharge.

(c) Wherefore, the plaintiff claims against the defendants jointly and severally the total sum of US $689798.47 (equivalent of N16,729,009.51) as special and general damages for breach of contract and interest at the rate of 5% per annum on the judgment sum from the date of judgment until full satisfaction of judgment debt.

On the same date that the writ of summons was filed, a motion ex parte was also filed, praying the High Court "for the arrest and detention by the Sheriff of the Motor Vessel Vali P., pending any other order that the court may deem fit to make". The learned judge of the State High Court granted the prayer and adjourned the substantive suit and the motion on notice to a further date. On the 8th September, 1993, the appellant, (as plaintiff) filed another motion on notice dated 7th September, 1993 praying the court to transfer the suit and all processes filed in the case to the Federal High Court of Nigeria, Calabar Judicial Division. The motion was fixed for 15th September, 1993.

On the 14th September, 1993, the respondents (as defendants) filed a notice of preliminary objection, saying that the State High Court, Calabar, was incompetent to entertain or make any consequential order in the case, being an admiralty matter; that the suit from the State High Court constituted an attempt to expand the jurisdiction of the State High Court; and that since the State High Court lacked jurisdiction, it could not make any consequential orders.

ISSUE FOR DETERMINATION

Whether the State High Court as at September, 1993, had jurisdiction to hear and determine admiralty matters and if the answer is in the negative, what order can that court make; order for transfer or order for striking out?

HELD

"A cursory look at the writ of summons filed by the appellant before the State High Court of Cross River State, Calabar leaves no one in doubt that the claim is a claim in admiralty.

Since the claim of the appellant before the State High Court was filed in, September, 1993, and it is a claim in admiralty, I have no doubt in my mind that the state

High Court was incompetent to hear and determine the claim. I am also of the view that the only proper order that court can make in the circumstances is an order striking out the action", per **Obadina, JCA** at 61-62, para. H-A.

S. 251(1)(i) CITIZENSHIP AND VISAS

IN THE COURT OF APPEAL OF NIGERIA

CA/L/79/2003

MR. DANIEL ORHIUNU v. FEDERAL REPUBLIC OF NIGERIA

Citation: (2005) 1 NWLR (Pt. 906)39

Date: On Wednesday, the 14th day of July, 2004

FACTS

The Honourable Attorney General of the Federation, instituted proceedings against the appellant before the Federal High Court to grant the request of the United States of America for the extradition of the appellant to the United States of America for the offence of health care fraud, and aiding and abetting by the appellant. He was sentenced by Judge Edward C. Prado on 11/10/2001 in absentia at the United States District Court for the Western District of Texas to 87 months, 3 years supervised release, $1,061,110.55 in restitution and a special assessment of $300.

When the matter came up for the first time before Shuaibu J. on 28/10/ 2002, the appellant through his counsel raised a preliminary objection challenging the jurisdiction and competence of the Federal High Court to entertain the proceedings and a consequential order dismissing the request for his extradition to the United

States of America.

In his considered ruling on 25/11/2002, the learned trial judge held that the Federal High Court has exclusive jurisdiction in extradition matters and consequently dismissed the appellant's preliminary objection.

ISSUE FOR DETERMINATION

Whether having regard to the wordings of section 251 (1)(i) of the Constitution of the Federal Republic of Nigeria 1999, the Federal High Court can be said to be conferred with jurisdiction or exclusive jurisdiction in respect of extradition of Nigerians from Nigeria to foreign countries?

HELD

"The provisions of section 251(1)(i) are clear and unambiguous. The subject matter in respect of which the Federal High Court shall have jurisdiction includes extradition. The section as it is without the addition of the word "of" is very clear, intelligible and unambiguous so as to convey the intention of the lawmakers in conferring jurisdiction on the Federal High Court in respect of extradition matters. This subsection (i) of section 251 is not the only subsection that is not introduced with the words like "relating to", "connected with," "arising from". The other subsections with no such introductory words but which are still unambiguous are section 251(1)(j), (k), (I), (m), (n) and (0)," per **Galadima, JCA** page 54, para. E-G.

S. 251(1)(k) Carriage by air

In the Supreme Court of Nigeria

SC.217/2004

CAMEROON AIRLINES v. MR. MIKE E. OTUTUIZU

Citation: (2011) 4 NWLR (Pt. 1238) Page 512

Date: On Friday, the 4th day of February, 2011

FACTS

The respondent as plaintiff sued the appellant, as defendant in the Federal High Court, Lagos Division, claiming in paragraph 15 of his statement of claim thus:

> 15. WHEREFORE the plaintiff claims the sum of N5,000,000.00 (five million naira) from the defendant being general and special damages as follows:

(A) Special Damages

Particulars of special damages:

(i) Cost of ticket i.e. 923 US dollars or its naira equivalent N80.000.00

(ii) The sum of 20,000.00 US dollars or its naira equivalent, removed from the defendant and unrefunded till date ...N1,800,000.00

(iii) Cost of sundry personal effect removed by the

defendant from the plaintiff N200, 000.00

(B) General Damages - N1.920.000 00

Total - N5,000,000 00

The plaintiff gave evidence in support of his case and tendered three exhibits, viz Exhibits A and B, airline tickets issued by the defendant, Exhibit C, receipt for foreign currency $20,000 00.

An employee of the defendant gave evidence for the defendant. In a considered judgment delivered on the 23rd of June 2000, the learned trial judge, Sanyaolu J. (as he then was) concluded thus:

> In conclusion, I hereby enter judgment for the plaintiff against the defendant in the sum of N580,000.00 (five hundred and eighty thousand naira) made up as follows:
>
> i. N80,000.00 being the cost of ticket
>
> ii. N500,000.00 as general damages
>
> Total N580,000.00

The defendant appealed, and the plaintiff cross appealed to the Court of Appeal.

ISSUE FOR DETERMINATION

Whether the subject matter of this action being one of international carriage of passengers and goods by air is not exclusively governed by the Warsaw Convention 1955 (applicable in Nigeria by virtue of the Colonies Protectorates and Trust Territories Order 1953, Vol. XI of the 1958 Laws of the Federation of Nigeria), within the exclusive jurisdiction of the Federal High Court?

HELD

The Federal High Court has exclusive jurisdiction over Aviation related cases of action. See section 251(1)(K) of the Constitution; and a plaintiff, claimant would have a valid claim if his suit is commenced within two years from the date of arrival at his destination or from the date on which the aircraft ought to have arrived or from the date the flight ended. See Article 29 of both legislations." per **Bode Rhodes-Vivour, JSC** at pg. 537, para. G.

IN THE COURT OF APPEAL OF NIGERIA

CA/L/916/2007

NIGERIAN AVIATION HANDLING COMPANY LIMITED v. YINKA WORLD INVESTMENT LIMITED & ANOR

Citation: 3 iLAW /CA/L/916/2007

Date: On Monday, the 5th day of March, 2012

FACTS

The claims at the trial court, being the Lagos State High Court, filed by the respondent were as follows:

> The sum of N11.85 million being the value of four (a) cargoes belonging to the plaintiffs i.e. claimants, but lost through the negligent handling of the defendant and its agents through the breach of contract; ALTERNATIVELY.
>
> Delivery to the claimant of the four pieces of cargoes (sic) belonging to the claimants and containing a variety of high quality wristwatches.
>
> A sum of N7 million loss of profit or earning resulting from the loss of cargoes 10% interest per annum from the date of judgment until full payment of the judgment sum.

The defendant filed an amended statement of defence. It is the case of the appellant that the loss of his goods in the appellants warehouse at the Muritala Mohammed Airport on the 28th July 1999, arose from a contract of international transportation by air covered by airway bill. Judgment was given for the respondent. This led to the appeal since the appellant was dissatisfied.

ISSUES FOR DETERMINATION

- Whether in fact the Lagos State High Court has jurisdiction to adjudicate over this case?
- Whether there was simple contract of bailment between the appellant and the respondents separate and independent of the contract between the Ethiopian Airways and the respondents and whether the appellant is liable to the respondent in law?
- Whether the loss of goods in this case is a loss which occurred during the transportation of the goods by air and whether the loss is governed by the law on international transportation by air?

HELD

On the Jurisdiction of Lagos State High Court over the Subject Matter of the Action

1. I find as useful the submissions and agree with the respondent's learned counsel, when he submits that from the statement of claim of the respondent, then claimant, it was a clear one of bailment and cognizable by the Lagos State High court per **Danjuma, JCA** S. 251(1)(K) Carriage By Air.

On the subject matter of the claim

2. The appellant's amended statement of claim contained on page 74-77 of the record clearly shows that the appellant's claim at the trial High Court was one relating to bailment; and reference to the transportation of the goods by the Ethiopian Airways before delivery to the respondent for safe custody did not make it otherwise, per **Danjuma, JCA.**

IN THE COURT OF APPEAL OF NIGERIA
Holden in Benin

Suit No: CA/B/167/2005

UNITED PARCEL SERVICE v. KOSOKO ADEYOSOYE

Citation: (2010) LPELR-CA/B/167/2005

Date: On Friday, the 9th day of July, 2010

FACTS

In the Federal High Court Benin, the respondent as the plaintiff brought a claim against the appellant as defendant alleging that he paid the appellant, a courier company, N12,685 for delivery of two parcels abroad. The respondent further alleged that the appellant failed to deliver one of the parcels to the recipient abroad and claimed four million naira as general damages as well as special damage in the sum of N12,685 only. Judgment was given for the plaintiff. The defendant appealed and raised the issue of jurisdiction of the Federal High Court.

ISSUE FOR DETERMINATION

Whether the trial Federal High Court had jurisdiction to try the suit?

HELD

"The claim is simply an issue of contract between the

appellant and respondent.

It is the obligation of the appellant to deliver the letter handed over to him at a particular destination. The manner of transportation of the letter is not the business of the respondent.

The respondent has no contract with any airline nor is he privy to the manner of transportation. The subject matter of the claim is a 'letter' which cannot be classified as baggage or cargo.

The Federal High Court has exclusive jurisdiction in matters listed in section 251(1) of the Constitution of Nigeria 1999. All other items not set out in the section is outside the jurisdiction of the Federal High court. It will be within the competence of the State High Court.

In other words, simple contract is not one of the matters placed exclusively within the jurisdiction of the Federal High Court," per **Shoremi, JCA.**

In the Court of Appeal of Nigeria

Division

CA/K/273/95

EGYPT AIR v. ALHAJI UMARU TA'AMBU ABDULLAHI

Citation: (1997) NWLR (Pt. 528) 179

Date: On Thursday, the 22nd day of May, 1997

FACTS

The respondent who was the plaintiff took out a writ of summons at the High Court of Kano State dated 25th October, 1990 and claimed the total sum of N378,024.00 from the appellant which was the defendant, being the total value of textile materials and threads entrusted by the plaintiff to the defendant for freight by air from Cairo in Egypt to Kano in Nigeria and general damages. Judgment was entered for the plaintiff. The defendant appealed against the decision of the trial court.

ISSUE FOR DETERMINATION

Whether the trial court, a State High Court had jurisdiction to entertain and give judgment in the suit?

HELD

It is quite clear from the provisions of S. 230(1)(k) of the 1979 Constitution as amended by Decree 107 of 1993, S. 251(1)(k) of 1999 Constitution) and S.7(1)(1) of the Federal High Court Act as amended by Decree No. 60 of 1991 which came into force on 26/8/93, that jurisdiction in respect of actions and matters on aviation and safety of aircraft and carriage of passengers and goods by air and meteorology, is vested exclusively in the Federal High Court to the exclusion of any other court, irrespective of whatever it is contained in the 1979 Constitution as amended,"per **Mohammed, JCA** at page 188, para. E–F.

IN THE COURT OF APPEAL OF NIGERIA
Division

CA/K/199/95

SUDAN AIRWAYS COMPANY LIMITED v. SURAJO MOHAMMED ABDULLAHI

Citation: [1998] 1 NWLR (Part 532)156

Date: On Thursday, the 27th day of November, 1997

FACTS

The respondent (as plaintiff) at the High Court of Kano State, claimed from the appellant (as defendant) the sum of N300,000.00 (Three hundred thousand naira only) being cost of kola nut consigned to the appellant, an airline company engaged in the freight of goods and passengers to several countries of the world including Nigeria, having its regional office at Post Office Road, Kano, for delivery at Khartoum, Sudan. This consignment was never delivered at Khartoum to the respondent as agreed upon by the parties.

ISSUE FOR DETERMINATION

Whether as at 1994 which was when the learned trial judge entertained the respondent's claim and gave judgment in favour of the respondent, he had the jurisdiction to determine issues arising from a contract of carriage of goods and passengers by air?

HELD

Since the claim of the respondent at the lower court related to carriage of goods and passengers by air, the lower court certainly had no jurisdiction as at the time it entertained the matter. The best course opened to the lower court was to transfer the matter to the Federal High Court, Kano. See section 7(6)(b) of Decree 60 of 1991. But as the lower court did not comply with this provision, I have no alternative to declare the whole proceeding including the judgment of the lower court a nullity," **Muhammad, JCA** at page 164, para. G-H.

Drugs and poisons S. 251(1)(m)

In the Court of Appeal

Ilorin Judicial Division

Suit No: CA/IL/C.35/2012

STANLEY OSSAI v. THE FEDERAL REPUBLIC OF NIGERIA

Citation: (2012) LPELR-19669(CA)

Date: On Monday, the 29th day of October, 2012

Appellant was charged at the Federal High Court Ilorin, on 24th February, 2012 as follows:

> That you STANLEY OSSAI, male, adult, 34 years, on the 6th day of February, 2012 at Oyun area in Ilorin East Local Government Area of Kwara State, within the jurisdiction of this honourable court, without lawful authority dealt in 10 kilograms of *Cannabis sativa,* otherwise known (sic) as Indian hemp a drug similar to cocaine, heroin, LSD, etc. thereby committing an offence contrary to and punishable under section 11(c) of the National Drug Law Enforcement Agency Act, "Cap N30 Laws of the Federation of Nigeria, 2004." On being arraigned on 15th March, 2012 he pleaded guilty to the charge and was convicted and sentenced to 2years imprisonment, starting from 6th February, 2012,

by Hon. Justice A.O. Faji who heard the case. The accused however appealed against the conviction.

ISSUE FOR DETERMINATION

Whether the learned trial court was right in assuming jurisdiction in the case, convicting and sentencing the appellant for offence of dealing in 10 kilograms of *Cannabis sativa,* otherwise known as Indian hemp?

HELD

On the exclusive jurisdiction of the Federal High Court over drugs/poisons under section 251(1) (M) And (2) of The 1999 Constitution.

> The National Drug Law Enforcement Agency Act, Cap N30, Laws of the Federation of Nigeria, 2004, which, in section 26(1) thereof, donates jurisdiction to the lower court over the charge leveled against the appellant, traces its potency to the provision of section 251(1)(m) and (2) of the 1999 Constitution, as amended. The latter provision allots to the lower court the power to entertain criminal matters relating to drugs and poisons which *Cannabis sativa,* the drug he was accused to have unlawfully dealt with, legitimately belongs. The constitution, as amended, occupies a kingly position in the corpus of our jurisprudence and its provisions are not only sacrosanct, but override any other prescription of any other law that is antithetical to it," per **Obande Ogbuinya, JCA.**

IN THE COURT OF APPEAL
(Ilorin Judicial Division)

Suit No: CA/IL/C.38/2012

NURA OCHALA v. FEDERAL REPUBLIC OF NIGERIA

Citation: (2013) LPELR-21386(CA)

Date: On Wednesday, the 19th day of June, 2013

FACTS

The National Drug Law Enforcement Agency, Kwara State Command, acting for the Attorney General of the Federation, arraigned the appellant before the Federal High Court Ilorin on 9th November, 2011, for dealing with Indian hemp without lawful authority. The appellant pleaded guilt and was convicted. However he appealed against the decision.

ISSUE FOR DETERMINATION

> Whether by virtue of the express provisions of the Indian hemp Act, volume 7, Cap. 16, Laws of the Federation of Nigeria, 2004, the Federal High Court was right to have assumed jurisdiction to try, convict and sentence the appellant herein, for an Indian hemp related offence?

HELD

"Now, the sacrosanct provision of section 251(1)(m) of the constitution, as amended, donates exclusive jurisdiction to the Federal High Court (the lower court) on civil cases and matters relating to drugs and poisons", per **Obande Festus Ogbuinya.**

IN THE COURT OF APPEAL OF NIGERIA

Division

Suit No: CA/IL/C.45/2012

DANJUMA RABE v. FEDERAL REPUBLIC OF NIGERIA

Citation: (2013) LPELR-20163(CA)

Date: On Thursday, the 7th day of February, 2013

FACTS

On 21st March, 2012, the appellant, a 27year-old labourer, was a passenger in a motor vehicle that was searched at Bode-Saadu, Jebba Road, in Moro Local Government of Kwara State by officers of the National Drug Law Enforcement Agency, Kwara State Command. In the course of that search, the officers found on the appellant dried weeds, suspected to be Indian hemp, otherwise known as *Cannabis sativa.*

Consequently, the appellant was arrested by those officers. After the preliminary investigation and field tests, the National Drug Law Enforcement Agency, Kwara State Command, acting for the Attorney General of the Federation, arraigned the appellant before the lower court on 22nd March, 2012. The charge, a one-count charge, found on page 1 of the printed record, was to the effect that the appellant: "without lawful authority trafficked in 4.4 kilogrammes of *Cannabis sativa* otherwise know (sic) as Indian hemp, a drug similar to cocaine, heroin, LSD, etc. thereby committing (sic), an offence contrary to and punishable under section 11 (b) of the National Drug Law Enforcement Agency Act Cap N30 Laws of the Federation of Nigeria 2004."

On that date of arraignment before the lower court, 22nd May, 2012, the charge was read, interpreted and explained to the appellant from English to Hausa and vice versa and he pleaded guilty to it. Sequel to that guilty plea, the respondent, without objection, fielded Pw1, Ahmed Akopari Suleiman, an exhibit keeper in the Kwara State Command of the agency who presented the facts of the case to the lower court. In the course of his evidence, Pw1 tendered all the necessary documentary evidence which were, without opposition, admitted in evidence as exhibits A, B, C, D, E, F, G and H and H1. The appellant had no questions for the Pw1 under cross-examination after his evidence. Thereafter, the respondent urged the lower court, without objection, to convict the appellant based on the evidence. Thereupon, the lower court convicted the appellant as charged. The accused appealed against the conviction.

ISSUE FOR DETERMINATION

Whether the Federal High Court has jurisdiction to try the appellant for the offence of trafficking 4.4 kg of *Cannabis sativa* (Indian hemp) having regard to the provision of the Constitution of the Federal Republic of Nigeria, 1999, National Drug Law Enforcement Agency Cap N30, Laws of the Federation of Nigeria 2004 and the

Indian hemp Act Cap 116 of the Laws of the Federation 2004?

HELD

"The Federal High Court shall also have and exercise jurisdiction and power in respect of criminal cases and matters, in respect of which jurisdiction is conferred by subsection (1) of the section." See *Abbas v. C.O.P* (1998) 12 NWLR (Pt. 577) 308. Interestingly, the Supreme Court has given its imprimatur to the fact that Indian hemp is a drug within the meaning of drugs in section 11 of the National Drug Law Enforcement Agency Act in the recent case of *Okewu v. FRN* (2012) 9 NWLR (Pt. 1305) 327. It stems from these highlights that the Constitution, as amended, has made clear and copious provisions in allotting jurisdiction to the Federal High Court over criminal cases and matters touching on Indian hemp. Indubitably, the Federal High Court traces the statutory paternity of its jurisdiction over Indian hemp offences, allocated to it by section 26(1) of the National Drug Law Enforcement Agency Act, to the Constitution, as amended," per **Ogbuinya, JCA.**

MINING S. 251(1)(n)

IN THE SUPREME COURT OF NIGERIA

Suit No: SC.244/2001

ALPHONSUS NKUMA v. JOSEPH OTUNUYA ODILI & ORS

Citation: (2006) 6 NWLR (Pt. 977)

Date: On Friday, the 10th day of March, 2006

FACTS

Between 1975 and 1976, the Nigerian Agip Oil Company Limited (hereinafter described as AGIP) deposited in the office of the Divisional Officer, Oguta, the sum of twenty-five thousand, one hundred and eighty naira, thirty-two kobo (N25,180.32k). The money was intended as compensation for the use of the parcel of land now in dispute by AGIP which was using the land for its oil operations. The money was to be paid to the owners of the land. This deposit led to the present dispute. The plaintiff and the defendant respectively claimed that they were each entitled to the compensation as owner of the land, to the exclusion of the other.

The plaintiff's suit was filed in 1977 and the defendant's in 1978. Both actions were consolidated. Judgment was delivered by the trial judge on 11/12/97.

An appeal was lodged at the Court of Appeal by the plaintiff and same was dismissed. The appellant appealed further to the Supreme Court.

ISSUE FOR DETERMINATION

Whether considering the provisions of Decree 60 of 1991 and Decree 107 of 1993, (which amended S. 230(1) of the 1979 Constitution by conferring exclusive jurisdiction to try civil cases and matters connected with or pertaining to mines and minerals including oil fields on the Federal High Court) the Court of Appeal was right in holding that the Imo State High Court was seized with jurisdiction to hear and determine the cases in point?

HELD

> I think that appellant's counsel has stretched beyond reasonable limit, the meaning to be ascribed to the expression connected with or appertaining to mines and minerals including oil fields. All the cases in which the Court of Appeal and this Court had decided that the provisions of both decrees ousted the jurisdiction of a State High Court clearly touched on issues of compensation for pollution and damages resulting from mining operations and related matters, and none was on compensation for owners of the land. This case is simply a land dispute. It could well have been a land dispute as to who was entitled to the compensation for a land to be used for farming, golfing or a football field, per **Oguntade, JSC** at page 602, para. E-G.

In the Supreme Court of Nigeria

Suit No: SC.9/1999

THE SHELL PETROLEUM DEVELOPMENT COMPANY OF NIGERIA LIMITED v. CHIEF G.B.A. TIEBO & ORS

Citation: (2005) 9 NWLR (Pt. 931) 439

Other Citations: (2005) 9 MJSC 158

Date: On Friday, the 8th day of April, 2005

FACTS

The respondents, as the plaintiffs, commenced their suit on 6th June, 1988 at the Yenagoa High Court of Rivers State claiming against the defendant for the sum of sixty four million, one hundred and forty six thousand naira being special and general damages for the negligence of the defendant and for allowing crude oil, which the defendant was mining, to spill into the lands, swamps, creeks, ponds, lakes and shrines of the plaintiffs. The plaintiffs sued for themselves and as the representatives of the Peremabiri Community in YELGA. The parties filed and exchanged pleadings after which the suit was heard by Blankson J. In all, the plaintiffs called nine witnesses in support of their case. The defendant called three. At the conclusion of hearing, the learned trial judge in his judgment on 27/2/91 awarded in the plaintiffs' favour, general damages totalling six million naira and one million naira costs. Dissatisfied with the judgment of the trial court, the defendant brought an appeal before the Court of Appeal, Port-Harcourt Division (hereinafter referred to as 'the court below'). On 27th March, 1996, the court below in its judgment dismissed the appeal. The defendant has come before the Supreme Court on a further appeal.

ISSUE FOR DETERMINATION

Was the judgment of the court below ultra vires?

HELD

Exclusive Jurisdiction of the Federal High Court over Mining oil, etc. Under the 1999 Constitution

1. Under Decree No.107 of 1993, the jurisdiction to adjudicate on mines and minerals and allied matters was given exclusively to the Federal High Court. This remained the position before the 1999 Constitution came into force. Under section 251(1) of the 1999 Constitution, the Federal High Court now possesses and exercises exclusive jurisdiction in "mines and minerals (including oil fields, oil mining, geological surveys and natural gas per **Oguntade, JSC** at page 459-460, para. H-B

On the law existing when the cause of action arose

2. In the instant case, the cause of action accrued to the plaintiffs on 16th January, 1987 and they

commenced their suit on 6th June, 1988. Judgment was delivered on 27th February, 1991. On these various dates, a State High Court had jurisdiction to entertain matters and cases on mines and minerals and oil fields. It is settled that the law applicable to an action is the law existing when the cause of action arose. See *Uwaifo v. Attorney General, Bendel State* (1983) NCLR 1 and *Adesina v. Kola* (1993) 6 NWLR (Pt. 298) 182 at 185.

The result is that the Rivers State High Court had jurisdiction to entertain the plaintiffs' suit and that jurisdiction was not in any way impaired between the commencement of the action on 6th June 1988 and the delivery of judgment on 27th February, 1991," per **Oguntade, JSC** at page 460 para. B-D

In the Supreme Court of Nigeria

Suit No: SC.75/1997

SHELL PET. DEV. CO. NIG. LTD v. ISAIAH

Citation: (2001) 11 NWLR (Pt. 723)168

Date: On Friday, the 18th day of May, 2001

FACTS

In July, 1988 an old tree fell on the appellant's oil pipeline and indented it, thereby obstructing the free flow of crude oil. The oil pipeline was owned and controlled by the appellant and ran across the respondents' swampland and surrounding farmlands. The appellant engaged the services of a contractor to repair the dented pipeline. In the cause of the repairs, crude oil freely spilled onto the respondents' swampland. The spillage quickly spread over the respondents' communally owned "Miniabia" swampland and polluted the surrounding farmlands, streams and fish ponds.

The respondents brought an action against the appellant before the Rivers State High Court, sitting at Isiokpo. At the said trial court, the plaintiffs, who are respondents in this appeal, claimed from the defendant (appellant in this appeal) for the following reliefs:

(a) The sum of N22 million being fair and reasonable compensation due and payable to the plaintiffs by the defendant for the permanent damage and loss to the plaintiffs' plant, marine and domestic life which was caused by the defendant's oil exploration activities whereby the defendant's oil pipes were caused by the defendant to open up in 1988 and caused extensive oil spillage and pollution and the said pollution has remained continuous at the plaintiffs' "Miniabia" land and water forest swampland at Omuoda, Aluu, within the jurisdiction of the honourable court, etc.

The trial court gave judgment for the plaintiffs. The court of Appeal affirmed the decision of the trial court. The appellant was dissatisfied with the decision of the trial court, hence appealed to the Supreme Court.

ISSUE FOR DETERMINATION

Was the court below right in holding that the trial court had jurisdiction to try the case?

HELD

1. "It is clear from the pleadings that the spillage and pollution occurred when the appellant was trying to repair the indented pipeline by cutting off the said section and installing a new section. I think it cannot be disputed if I say that installation of pipelines, producing, treating and transmitting of crude oil to the storage tanks is part of petroleum mining operations. Therefore, if an incident happens during the transmission of petroleum to the storage tanks, it can be explained as having arisen from or

connected with or pertaining to mines and minerals, including oil fields, and oil mining. I, therefore, agree that the subject matter of the respondents' claim falls within the exclusive jurisdiction of the Federal High Court as is provided under section 230(1)(a) of Constitution (Suspension and Modification) Decree No. 107. Similar opinions concerning claims pertaining to oil spillage have been held by the Court of Appeal in *Barry and 2 Ors v. Obi A. Eric and 3 Ors* (1998) 8 NWLR (pt. 562) 404 at 416 and *The Shell Petroleum Development Company* of *Nigeria Limited v. Otelemaba Maxon and Ors* (2001) 9 NWLR (pt. 719) 541," per **Mohammed,** at 179, para. C-E.

2. "The trial of the action was in progress when Decree 107 of 1993 (*contains provisions which are impari material with S. 251(1)(n) of the 1999 Constitution*) was signed into law. From that moment when the Decree was signed into Law, the jurisdiction of the State High Court to determine any matter connected with or pertaining to mining and minerals, including oil fields, oil mining, geological surveys and natural gas has been ousted. Once the jurisdiction of a court to determine a matter has been ousted, any further hearing in the matter is indeed null and void because any decision it makes amounts to nothing," per **Mohammed, JSC** at Page 179, para. G-H.

IN THE COURT OF APPEAL OF NIGERIA

PORT HARCOURT DIVISION

CA/PH/43/2012

MOBIL PRODUCING NIGERIA UNLIMITED v. SUFFOLK PETROLEUM SERVICES LIMITED

Citation: (2013) LPELR-21193(CA)

Date: On Wednesday, the 20th day of February, 2013

FACTS

The respondent in this appeal as plaintiff (claimant) in the lower court commenced proceedings in that court claiming some declaratory reliefs, and injunctions against the appellants as defendants in respect of a contract between the parties.

The respondent also filed an ex parte motion for interim injunction.

When the ex parte motion for interim injunction came up before the lower court, on the 25/6/11, the court, after granting leave for service of the defendant outside jurisdiction, ordered the defendant to appear before it on 1/11/11 to show cause why an order of interim injunction should not be made. Upon service on it of the process of court including the order to show cause aforesaid, the appellant (defendant in the court below) filed an application for stay of the proceedings of the lower court pending arbitration between the parties pursuant to the terms of their contract. Both the motion for stay of proceedings and the one for interim injunction came up before the lower court on 1/11/11 and that court granted the application for interim injunction and adjourned the motion for stay of proceedings to 22/11/11 for hearing. The present appeal is against that ruling.

ISSUE FOR DETERMINATION

Whether the Federal High Court has the jurisdiction to entertain the respondent's matter and to make the order of interim injunction pertaining to simple contracts?

HELD

"The subject matter of the action which gave rise to the claims was set out in paragraph 9 of the statement of claim. That paragraph reads as follows:

> 9. Under the said subcontract, even though the scope of work shall be as defined in individual Letters of Authorisation (LOAs) issued under the subcontract, the subcontract is generally described as offshore pipeline installation engineering, procurement, construction and installation work for the defendant's Major Integrity Projects (MIPS), offshore Nigeria.

However, the scope of work expected to be carried out under the subcontract include:

- shore crossings;
- onshore pipeline sections;

- the fabrication and installation of associated risers;
- pig launchers and receivers;
- pump and air compressor skids; and deck extensions, as well as execution of the tie ins, the in-place abandonment of existing pipeline segment, removal of existing risers, etc."

Section 251(1) of the 1999 Constitution clearly places the matter listed in subsection (1)-(a), (b) within the exclusive jurisdiction of the Federal High Court. Subsection (1)(n) is relevant to the present proceedings on appeal before us. It reads:

> (1)(n) Mines and minerals (including oil fields, oil mining, geological surveys and natural gas).

This portion of section 251 of the Constitution has been subject to numerous judicial interpretations and dicta by the Courts. In *Shell Petroleum Dev. Co. Nig. Ltd v. Isaiah* (2001) 11 NWLR (pt. 723) 168 at 178-180, the Supreme Court held that the construction, operation and maintenance of an oil pipeline are matters pertaining to or connected with mines and minerals, including oil fields, oil mining, etc. as envisaged under section 251(1)(n) of the Constitution and therefore within the exclusive jurisdiction of the Federal High Court. Similar conclusions were reached in the principle of the decisions in *Barry v. Eric* (1998) 8 NWLR (Pt. 562) 404 at 417 and 422-423 and the views of Saulawa JCA in *SPDC v. SIRPI Alusteel Construction Ltd* (supra) at page 163 with which view I agree. See also *Shell Petroleum Dev. Co. of Nig. Ltd v. Maxon* (2001) 9 NWLR (Pt. 719) 541 at 554-555.

From the above postulations of the law on the matter, it is clear to my mind and I do not have the slightest doubt that the pleading in the statement of claim particularly paragraph 9 thereof which distinctly set put the scope of the contract, brings the action squarely within the provisions of section 251(1)(n) of the Constitution thus fixing exclusive jurisdiction in the action in the Federal High Court which the lower court is. Accordingly, my answer on the first issue is in the affirmative. The lower court therefore had jurisdiction", per **Nwosu-Iheme, JCA.**

S. 251(1)(o) Weights and measures

In the Court of Appeal of Nigeria

Calabar Division

CA/C/136/2001

FEDERAL MINISTRY OF COMMERCE AND TOURISM & ANOR v. CHIEF BENEDICT EZE

Citation: (2006) All FWLR (Pt. 323) 1704

Other Citation: (2005) LPELR-CA/C/136/2001

Date: On Tuesday, the 14th day of June, 2005

FACTS

For an alleged violation of the Weights and Measures Act, the appellant impounded the respondent's facilities including a Yamaha generator, some petrol, diesel and kerosene, nozzles from the respondent's filling station for alleged unlawful manipulation of the gauge and meters, in violation of Weights and Measures Act (CAP 467) Laws of the Federation of Nigeria 1990. The respondent brought an action for the enforcement of his fundamental rights at the State High Court in Calabar. The appellant brought a motion to set aside the interim order made by the court. The application was refused. The trial court also held that it had jurisdiction to hear the matter since the action was brought pursuant to the fundamental human rights enforcement rules. The appellant was aggrieved and appealed to the Court of Appeal.

ISSUES FOR DETERMINATION

Whether or not having regard to the nature of the motion ex parte and parties involved, a State High Court is seized with jurisdiction to entertain the suit?

HELD

On Exclusive Jurisdiction of the Federal High Court in Respect of Subject Matters Listed Under S. 251(1) of the 1999 Constitution.

1. "one of the principles developed on the point from the decided cases is that in their interpretation or application of section 251 on the exclusive jurisdiction of the Federal High Court, the courts construe the said provision strictly or even technically and they confine themselves in that sense only to the specific subjects or subject matters contained in the section. Thus, any other matter or subject not specifically mentioned under or in the provision of the section are regarded as excluded from the jurisdiction of the Federal High Court. There is also a proviso under the section which is applied or relied upon by the courts in appropriate cases to whittle down or curtail the jurisdiction of the Federal High Court (even where the matter is specifically

mentioned in the provision) in respect of cases for claim, of damages, injunction or specific performance where the action is based on any enactment law or equity. See *IGP v. Algbiremolun* (supra); *Okafor* v. *Hashim* (supra); *NDIC v. FMBN* (1997) 2 NWLR (Pt. 490) 735; *Hon Minister of Works & Housing v. Tomas Nigeria Ltd* & *Ors* (supra); *NNPC v. Okwor* (1998) 7 NWLR (Pt. 559) 637; *NIDB v. Fenibol Nig. Ltd* (1997) NWLR (Pt. 489) 543; *Garba v. FCSC* (1988) 1 NWLR (Pt. 71) 449; and *Odutola v. University of Ilorin* (2004) 12 SCN 236 at 251-252.

The provision to S. 251 of the 1999 Constitution has been applied in a number of decided cases as can be seen from the above cited ones amongst others. Our first step in the application of the principle established in the above cited cases is therefore to find out whether the subject or subject matter in the present case is one of those expressly mentioned or listed in any of the paragraphs in section 251 in which case the Federal High Court will assume jurisdiction or will be the proper court with the requisite jurisdiction to hear and determine the application. It will be recalled here that the appellants in their brief have stated the basis for their action in the seizure of the respondent's pumping machine and other properties which they asserted was done in accordance with the Weights and Measures Act (supra). They alleged that they have the power to make the seizure where they find on inspection that a petrol dealer has altered his pumping machine. The respondent has not replied on this point throughout his brief of argument;

consequently, the appellants' assertion must be accepted as un-contradicted.

Accordingly, if a closer look is made to the subjects under section 251, it would easily be seen that the appellants' action is covered under section 251(1)(o) which provides expressly for "weights and measures" making it one of the matters or cases for which the Federal High Court can exercise exclusive jurisdiction. Moreover, by paragraphs 251(1)(r), the Federal High Court also has jurisdiction, subject to the provision of the Constitution, in cases involving the Federal Government or any of its agencies or in proceedings for declaration or injunction affecting the validity of any executive action or decision by the Federal Government or any of its agencies.

It is my humble view that the appellants in the instant case are, as their names suggest, an agencies or agents of the Federal Government charged with the enforcement of all the sanctions under the Weights and Measures Act and were therefore performing an administrative or executive function (of seizure) on behalf of or as agents of the said Federal Government. It is, therefore, my view that the present ease should have been filed at the Federal High Court which has an exclusive jurisdiction to hear and determine it under section 251(1) (o), (q) and (r). This is what the Supreme Court decided in both *NEPA v. Adegbero* (supra) and *Odutola v. Unilorin* (supra)," per **Adamu, JCA** at 1720-1721, para. C-E.

Where the reliefs sought against an agency of the Federal Government is injunctive or declarative affecting the validity of its effective actions

2. "In applying the above principles on the issue of jurisdiction to the facts and circumstances of the present case, it will be easily seen that by reference to the respondent's claims as per the reliefs set out at page 2 of the record of proceedings (which are also repeated at page 4 thereof), the said respondent sought for a declaration and other injunctive orders on or affecting the validity or otherwise of the administrative actions or decisions of the appellants who were agents of the Federal Government. Consequently, the action is aptly caught by and comes within the purview of section 251(1)(s) of the 1999 constitution for which the Federal High Court is vested with an exclusive jurisdiction - see *NNPC v. Okwor* (1998) 7 NWLR (Pt. 559) 637 and *Minister of Works v. Tomas Nig. Ltd* (supra) (at Pt. 788) of the report. Moreover, when the above conditions for the court's exercise of jurisdiction are applied on the trial High Court, it will be seen by reference to section 251(1)(s) and the Weights and Measures Act (supra) that the subject matter of the litigation or dispute is not, or does not fall within its jurisdiction and that there is a factor inhibiting or preventing its exercise of jurisdiction (i.e. the conferment or vesting of exclusive jurisdiction on the Federal High court under section 251(1)(o) of the Constitution.

It is clear that the appropriate court to deal with such matter or to adjudicate in such matter by virtue of the constitutional provision and the Act (supra) is the Federal High Court. Consequently, the trial court in the present case being a state High Court has been divested of and lacked the requisite jurisdiction to adjudicate or to hear and determine the respondent's application" per **Dalhatu Adamu, JCA** at 1724, para. A-E

PART 3

Jurisdiction of the Federal High Court in Actions Involving the Federal Government or Her Agencies as Well as Criminal Cases and Matters Related to S. 251(1)

The most ubiquitous attacks on the jurisdiction of high courts arising from the provisions of section 251 of the 1999 Constitution are most often provoked when an agency of the Federal Government is made a party to the suit. A preliminary objection to the jurisdiction of a court to try a matter can be lethal, if the plaintiff misconceives the principles that may operate to determine the position of the court in various circumstances. Section 251(1)(p), (q) and (r) and the proviso to paragraph (r) of the constitution, have proved critical in the determination of such objections.

Many cases involving disputes over the jurisdiction of the Federal High Court as against the State High Court also call for the consideration of section 251(3) of the said Constitution which provides that,

> The Federal High Court shall also have and exercise jurisdiction and powers in respect of criminal cases and matters, in respect of which jurisdiction is conferred by subsection (1) of this section.

The cases below present a synopsis of the current attitude of the appellate courts when the jurisdiction to try matters involving agencies of the Federal Government as well as criminal cases wherein items listed in section 251(1) of the Constitution are in issue. Some of the older cases here, illuminate the relevant principles from a historical perspective and are helpful in understanding the underlying rationale for the current position of the law.

Thus, this part is in two segments. Part 3A deals with the jurisdiction of the Federal High Court as against the State High Court in actions involving the Federal Government or her agencies, while Part 3B deals with section 251(3) of the 1999 Constitution which empowers the federal High Court to exercise jurisdiction in respect of matters listed in S. 251(1) of the said Constitution.

CHAPTER 6

PART 3 A

Jurisdiction of the Federal High Court as against the State High Court in actions involving the Federal Government or her agencies

As earlier indicated, the mere fact that the Federal Government or any of her agencies constitutes a party in a given suit does necessarily confer jurisdiction on the Federal High Court. The suit can only be initiated at the Federal High Court if the subject matter falls within the items enumerated in section 251(1) of the 1999 Constitution.

The following are notable cases which exemplify the above position of the law.

IN THE COURT OF APPEAL

LAGOS JUDICIAL DIVISION

Suit No: CA/L/171/01

PRINCE ALABI DOSUMU & ORS v. NIGERIAN NATIONAL PETROLEUM CORPORATION & ANOR

Citation: (2014) 6 NWLR (Pt. 1403) Page 282

Date: On Wednesday, the 17th day of April, 2013

FACTS

Appellants are the acclaimed principal members and accredited representatives of the Esimikan Family of Ilado-Odo and Inagbe-Odo villages, in the Ojo Local Government Area of Lagos State. The 1st respondent is a Federal Government Corporation responsible, inter alia, for the prospecting, drilling, marketing, *et al* of petroleum products in Nigeria.

The genesis of the instant appeal is traceable to December 20, 1993. That was the day the appellants instituted the suit in question against the respondents, vide a writ of summons and statement of claim in the lower court. By the statement of claim thereof, the appellants claim, inter alia, that sometime in 1977, the 1st respondent without the permission or consent of the appellants broke and entered into the appellants' land, situate and being at Inagbe-Odo, along the Badagry creeks, and laid petroleum pipelines therein. That the trespass still continued up to the date the action was filed on December 20, 1993.

Consequent upon the service of the originating processes, the 1st respondent filed a notice of preliminary objection challenging the competence of the suit. By the notice of preliminary objection, the 1st respondent urged upon the lower court to dismiss the suit on the five grounds including:

> (3) This honourable court is statutorily divested of the jurisdiction to entertain the subject matter of the suit.

The preliminary objection was upheld by the trial court. The plaintiff appealed against the ruling.

ISSUE FOR DETERMINATION

Whether the lower court was right to hold that it had no jurisdiction to entertain the suit?

HELD

"However, in my considered view, the crux of the issue goes beyond the mere question of whether the 1st respondent is an agency of the Federal Government. Indeed, the crux of the issue is whether the appellants' claim at the lower court comes within the purview of the proviso to section 251 (r) of Decree No. 107 of 1993 (now section 251(1) (p), (q) & (r) of the 1999 Constitution)."

The lower court has erred in abdicating jurisdiction in entertaining and determining the action before it. The simple reason being that, the appellants' claims, are exclusively and unambiguously for trespass to land, damages and injunction. Those claims, per se, do not relate to compulsory acquisition of land for which the proviso to section 251(1)(p), (q) & (r) (supra) is very much emphatical to the effect thus:

> Provided that nothing in the provisions of (p), (q) and (r) of this subsection shall prevent a person from seeking redress against the Federal Government or any of its agencies in an action for damages, injunction or specific performance where the action is based on any enactment, law or equity per. **Ibrahim Mohammed Musa Saulawa, JCA** at 308 para. B–D.

IN THE SUPREME COURT OF NIGERIA

Suit No: SC.224/2002

J.A. ADEKOYE AND ORS v. NIGERIAN SECURITY PRINTING AND MINTING COMPANY LTD

Citation: (2009) 5 NWLR (Pt. 1134) 322

Date: On Friday, the 6th day of February, 2009

FACTS

By an originating summons No. LD/M/358/92 filed on 25/6/92, the appellants as plaintiffs raised the following questions for determination by the Lagos State High Court:

(i) Whether the employees of the Nigerian Security Printing and Minting Company Limited (N.S.P.M.C) are public officers of the Federal Republic of Nigeria within the meaning of the Constitution of the Federal Republic of Nigeria, 1979.

(ii) Whether the Nigerian Security Printing and Minting Company Limited is part of the public service of the Federal Republic of Nigeria.

(iii) Whether the provisions of the Pensions Act, Cap 346 Laws of the Federation are applicable to the employees of N.S.P.M.C by virtue of being public officers of the Federation.

(iv) If the answer to question 3 is in the negative, whether as having been (sic) members of the public service of Nigeria and thereby made subject to the disabilities, liabilities and restrictions applicable to such officers the provisions of the Pensions Act which deprive them of some pension rights and privileges applicable to other public servants under that Act are not inconsistent with the constitution and therefore void.

The trial court held that the 1st defendant (Nigerian Security Printing Minting Company Limited) is part of the public service of the Federal Republic of Nigeria, yet entertained and granted the claims. The defendant appealed to the Court of Appeal which held that the said 1st defendant/appellant were made a part of the public service of the Federation under section 277 of the 1979 Constitution. However, that the provisions of the Pensions Act, Cap 346 do not apply to the plaintiffs/respondents. The plaintiffs appealed against the judgment, while the 1st defendant cross appealed on the issue of the jurisdiction of the trial Lagos State High Court to entertain the suit in the first place.

ISSUE FOR DETERMINATION

Whether in view of the provisions of section 230 of the

1979 Constitution,*(impari material with section 251 of the 1999 Constitution)* the Lagos State High Court has the jurisdiction to hear and determine the matter as constituted.

HELD

Status of a Company wherein the Federal Government Has Majority Shares

1. The said section 277(1) of the 1979 Constitution (*now S. 318 (1) of the 1999 Constitution)* defines "public service of the Federation" to mean "service of the Federation in any capacity in respect of the Government of the Federation and includes service as...

> (f) staff of any company or enterprise in which the Government of the Federation or its agency owns controlling share or interest; ....

From the above, it is very clear that by constitutional arrangement, the 1st respondent/cross appellant as well as its members of staff form part of the public service of the Federation and that the 1st respondent in particular is an agency of the Federal Government as it is not disputed that the Federal Government owns a controlling share in the 1st respondent/cross appellant.

I, therefore, hold the view that the 1st respondent/ cross appellant is an agency of the Federal Government contrary to the views of the lower court," per **W. S. N. Onnoghen, JSC** at page 341, para. H–page 342, para. B

Exclusive Jurisdiction of Federal High Court over Pension Dispute Concerning Federal Public Servants

2. "I therefore hold that the question of payment of pension to public servants or entitlement to payment of pension under the provisions of the Pensions Acts Cap 346, Laws of the Federation, 1990 is an issue within the administration, management and control of the 1st respondent/cross appellant within the provisions of section 230(1) of the 1979 Constitution (supra) and consequently that where an issue has arisen as in the instant case, between the 1st respondent and its staff or former employees, only the Federal High Court has the exclusive jurisdiction to hear and determine the dispute, not a state High Court," per **W. S. N. ONNOGHEN, JSC** at page 342, para. D– F.

IN THE SUPREME COURT OF NIGERIA

Suit No: SC.229/2004

AYODELE & ANOR. v AG FEDERATION

Citation: (2010) 15 NWLR (Pt. 1215) 169

Date: On Friday the 30th of April, 2010

FACTS

The appellants in this appeal were the plaintiffs at the Federal High Court Lagos where they, by a writ of summons and statement of claim, filed their action against the respondents herein who were the defendants and claimed against them in paragraph 13 of the statement of claim as follows:

(a) A declaration that they are the persons entitled to be issued with certificate of occupancy in respect of the various parcels of land being occupied by them and claimed by the first defendant at Yakoyo near Ojodu village.

(b) A declaration that the judgment in suit No. FHC/L/CS/820/95 is null and void as neither the plaintiffs nor the second and third defendants were served with court processes in the suit.

(c) An injunction restraining the defendants, their servants, agents privies and otherwise howsoever from interfering with the plaintiff's possession of

> the land being occupied by them at Yakoyo near Ojodu Village.

However, before the action came up for hearing, the 1st respondent who was the 1st defendant at the trial court filed a motion on notice urging the court to dismiss the action for want of jurisdiction to entertain the same. The 2nd respondent (Federal Ministry of Works and Housing) and 3rd respondent (Attorney General of the Federation), were respondents to the motion which was heard by the trial court. In its ruling delivered on 11th July, 2001, the trial court held that it has jurisdiction to entertain the plaintiffs' action by virtue of the provisions of section 251(1)(r) of the 1999 Constitution. The 1st respondent who was not happy with the ruling of the trial court decided to appeal against it to the Court of Appeal Lagos Division where the only issue raised for the determination of the appeal was:

> Whether by virtue of the provisions of section 251(1)(r) of the 1999 Constitution, the Federal High Court has jurisdiction to entertain an action for a declaration of title to the land.

After hearing the appeal, the Court of Appeal in resolving the single issue of jurisdiction that was placed before it for determination in its judgment delivered on 30th June, 2004 came to the conclusion that the provisions of section 251(1)(r) of the 1999 Constitution by virtue of which the trial court held that it has the required jurisdiction to entertain the plaintiffs/appellants' action, does not confer such jurisdiction on the trial court and consequently struck out the action in allowing the appeal. The plaintiffs who were not happy with that decision now appealed to the Supreme Court.

ISSUE FOR DETERMINATION

Whether or not the court below was right in its decision now on appeal that the trial court has no jurisdiction under section 251(1)(r) of the 1999 Constitution to entertain the plaintiffs/appellants' action claiming declaration of title to plots or parcels of land?

HELD

Where claim is for title to land

1. "It must be emphasised that the claims of the plaintiffs/appellants is for declaration of title to land and injunction to protect their possession of the land. The executive and administrative action or decision of the Federal Government and its agency, the Ministry of Works and Housing, to compulsorily acquire the parcels of land for public purposes namely, the construction of the Lagos–Ibadan Expressway is not at all the subject of the action. Thus, as the executive action of the Federal Government in compulsorily acquiring the land in dispute is not being challenged by the plaintiffs/appellants in their instant action, there is no opening whatsoever for the Federal High Court to come into the matter in exercise of its original jurisdiction

under section 251(1)(r) of the 1999 Constitution," per **M. Mohammed, JSC** at page 191 para. H– pg 192 para. C.

The Federal High Court Lacks Jurisdiction in Land Disputes irrespective of the Parties

2. "Close examination of the entire provisions of section 251 of the 1999 Constitution prescribing the jurisdiction of the Federal High Court to the exclusion of all other courts, there is nothing therein specifically conferring jurisdiction in that court in cases or matters concerning land disputes. Although the section also indicated that the National Assembly may confer additional jurisdiction to the court, there is no indication that such Act of the National Assembly had been promulgated conferring additional jurisdiction to the court to entertain cases and matters on land disputes", per **M. Mohammed, JSC** at Page 192 para. C-D.

3. "It is quite clear from the provisions of the above sections of the Land Use Act with specific powers and jurisdiction in respect of land matters specified therein conferred on State High Court, Area Court, Customary Court and Magistrate Court, that the Federal High Court is not one of the courts conferred with jurisdiction to entertain any dispute in land matters. In fact, the purpose which sections 39, 41 and 42 of the Land Use Act are designed to serve are very clear", per **M. Mohammed, JSC** at page 194 para. C-D.

In the Supreme Court of Nigeria

SC. 266/2006

ISAAC OBIUWEVBI v. CENTRAL BANK OF NIGERIA

Citation: (2011) All FWLR (pt. 575) page 208

Date: On Friday, the 11th day of March 2011

FACTS

The appellant was a senior employee of the respondent bank. On the 11th day of August, 1987 he was put on suspension, and on the 30th day of October, 1987 his appointment was terminated.

Aggrieved by the situation, he sued the respondent at the Lagos High Court. He sought a declaration that the decision to terminate his employment was unlawful, null, and void as it offends the rule of natural justice. He also claimed his entitlements and general damages in the sum of Nl00,000 against the respondent bank. The writ of summons and statement of claim were filed in the registry of the Lagos High Court on the 7th day of July, 1988. The suit was before Fafiade J (as she then was). Pending before the learned trial judge was a motion to dismiss the suit for want of jurisdiction. Reliance was placed on section 3 (3) of Decree No 17 of 1984.

On the 14th of April, 1989, the learned trial judge ruled that the Lagos High Court had jurisdiction to hear the case and adjourned hearing for the 25th and 26th of

October, 1989. Trial never commenced before Fafiade J. Her Lordship retired, and on the 22nd day of January, 1991, the case came before Olugbani J. (as he then was) for the first time. On the 15th of December, 1993, trial commenced with the appellant (as plaintiff) giving evidence. The plaintiff concluded his evidence on the 8th of October, 1996. No witnesses were taken thereafter, then on the 23rd of September, 2002, the case came before Lufadeju J (as she then was) for the first time.

The defendant/respondent brought a fresh preliminary objection challenging the jurisdiction of the State High Court in view of the provisions of section 251 (l)(p) and (r). The objection was upheld on 16th of December, 2003. The learned trial judge held that:

> By virtue of section 251(1) (p) and (r) of the 1999 Constitution, only the Federal High Court has exclusive jurisdiction in civil cases and matters pertaining (among other things) to the administrative action or decision of the Federal Government or any of its agencies.

And with the above reasoning, the learned trial judge ruled that the Lagos High Court lacks jurisdiction to hear the case and struck it out. The plaintiff (as appellant) appealed to the Court of Appeal. The court of appeal held thus;

> ..... In conclusion, I affirm the decision of the lower court in its ruling of 16th December, 2003 on the respondent's motion on notice. This appeal therefore fails.

Aggrieved, the appellant appealed to the Supreme Court.

ISSUE FOR DETERMINATION

Whether the High Court of Lagos had jurisdiction to hear and determine the suit which was brought before it by the appellant in view of the Constitution. (Suspension and Modification) Decree 107 of 1993 and the 1999 Constitution?

HELD

On the Exclusive Jurisdiction of the Federal High Court in Respect of the Administration, Management and Control of the Federal Government or any of Its agencies

In this appeal, it is not in dispute that the respondent, the Central Bank of Nigeria, is an agency of the Federal Government. Any lingering doubt of that fact is put to rest by the provisions of section 39 of the Central Bank of Nigeria Act, Cap 47 Laws of the Federation of Nigeria 1990 which states that the Central Bank may act generally as an agent for the Federal Government or of a state government. It is thus obvious that the respondent bank was established as an agency of the Federal Government. On subject matter of the litigation, the matter must arise from the administration, management and control of the Federal Government or any of its agencies, from the operation and interpretation of the Constitution and from any action or proceedings for a declaration or injunction affecting the validity of any executive or administrative action or decisions by the Federal Government, or any of its agencies.

I am firmly of the view that as from the 17th of November, 1993, the Federal High Court had exclusive jurisdiction if the matter is a civil matter arising from the administration, management and control of the Federal Government or any of its agencies. The matter must arise from the operation and interpretation of the constitution.

Finally, the matter must arise from any action or proceedings for a declaration or injunction affecting the validity of any executive or administrative action or decisions by the Federal Government, or any of its agencies", per **Bode Rhodes-Vivour JSC** at 228-229 para. F-A.

IN THE COURT OF APPEAL

KADUNA JUDICIAL DIVISION

CA/K/2007

NIGERIA UNITY LINE PLC v. USMAN

Citation: (2014) 6 NWLR (Pt. 1404) Page 546

Date: Tuesday, 7th May 2013

FACTS

The respondent commenced proceedings against the appellant for the recovery of the sum of USD 236,720.00 (two hundred and sixty-three thousand, seven hundred and twenty United States dollars) or its equivalent of N34,172,830,830.60 (thirty-four million, one hundred and seventy two thousand, eight hundred and thirty naira, sixty kobo) being his professional legal fees in respect of legal services rendered to the appellant and estacode allowance. The appellant is an agency of the Federal government. The suit was commenced at the Federal High Court, Kaduna.

The trial court found in favour of the respondent and awarded the prayers sought as per the writ of summons of the respondent.

Dissatisfied with the judgment of the trial court, the appellant appealed to the Court of Appeal challenging the jurisdiction of the Federal High Court to entertain the suit bordering on simple contract.

ISSUE FOR DETERMINATION

Whether the Federal High Court has jurisdiction to try the suit?

HELD

On Jurisdiction of the Federal High Court in Respect of Simple Contract

"I agree completely that this appeal succeeds on the ground of lack of jurisdiction on the part of the Federal High Court to entertain cases bordering on simple contract. This is clearly outside the purview of the provisions of section 251(1) of the 1999 Constitution of the Federal Republic of Nigeria which distinctly defined and limited the jurisdiction of the Federal High Court. See the Supreme Court case of *Felix Onuorah v. Kaduna Refining and Petrochemical Co. Ltd* (2005) 6 NWLR (Pt. 921) page 393 where it was enunciated that section 230(1) of the 1979 constitution as amended by Decree 107 of 1993 which is *in pari material* with the provisions of section 251(1) of the 1999 Constitution, does not confer the Federal High Court with jurisdiction over matters of simple contract. **Akitan JSC** in delivering the lead judgment said that section 230(1) provides a limitation to the general and all embracing jurisdiction of the Federal High Court because the items listed under the said section 230(1) can only be determined exclusively by the Federal High Court. All other items not included in the list would, therefore still be within the jurisdiction of the State High Court", per **Orji Abadua, JCA** at page 553, para. D-G.

In the Supreme Court of Nigeria

Holden at Abuja

SC.16/2013

OPIA v. INEC AND ANOR

Citation: (2014) 7 NWLR Page 413

Date: On Friday, 7th Feburay 2014

FACTS

The appellant contested election into the Imo State House of Assembly under the platform of the People's Democratic Party (PDP) to represent Ohaji/Egbema State Constituency during the 2011 general election held on 26th April 2011. The second respondent also contested the aforesaid election under the platform of the All Progressive Grand Alliance (APGA), with the 1st respondent herein, as umpire.

The election was inconclusive and therefore nullified by the 1st respondent. A supplementary election was held on 6th May 2011 which was won by the 2nd respondent who was declared the winner and issued a certificate of return by the 1st respondent. Accordingly, the 2nd respondent was sworn into the Imo State House of Assembly.

After the supplementary election and swearing in of the 2nd respondent into the Imo State House of Assembly, the appellant filed an originating summons before the Federal High Court, Owerri, challenging the conduct of the election, and the return of the 2nd respondent. The appellant sought inter alia, a declaration that having scored the majority of lawful votes cast in the election, conducted on the 26th of April 2011 and having been returned as the winner, it was unlawful, in the light of the provisions of section 68(1) **(C)** of the Electoral Act, 2010 (as amended), for the 1st respondent to conduct any supplementary election to elect another person in respect of the same position.

The second respondent filed a preliminary objection challenging the jurisdiction of the Federal High Court to entertain the appellant's claim. The preliminary objection was upheld on the ground that post election action came under the jurisdiction of the Election Petition Tribunal and not the Federal High Court.

The appeal filed against the above ruling by the appellant was dismissed. The appellant appealed to the Supreme Court.

ISSUE FOR DETERMINATION

Whether the jurisdiction of the Federal High Court in respect of the administrative action or decision of agencies of the Federal Government like INEC can be invoked to challenge the decision of INEC which returned a candidate as a winner at the election?

HELD

On the Degree and Range of the Exclusive Jurisdiction of the Federal High Court Under Section 251 of the 1999 Constitution.

"Though the reliefs sought by the appellant were for declarations and injunctions against the 1st respondent, an agency of the Federal Government, the main declaratory and injunctive reliefs prayed by the appellant were in respect of the supplementary election held on the 26th of April 2011; and the return of the 2nd respondent based on the result of the said supplementary election.

By section 251 of the 1999 Constitution, the eighteen main items enumerated therein do not include election matter.

Section 285(1)(d) of the 1999 Constitution, having specifically conferred the power to decide disputes arising from the conduct of election on the Election Tribunal, to the exclusion of regular courts, including the Federal High Court, the latter lacks the vires to decide election disputes", per **Galadima JSC** at 460 para. F–H.

IN THE SUPREME COURT OF NIGERIA

HOLDEN AT ABUJA

Suit No: SC.211/1999

PROFESSOR ADEREMI DADA OLUTOLA v. UNIVERSITY OF ILORIN

Citation: (2004) 18 NWLR (Pt. 905) 416

Date: On Friday, the 17th day of December, 2004

FACTS

The appellant commenced an action against the respondent on the 13th day of January, 1993 at the Kwara State High Court, seeking the following reliefs:

i. An order that the decision of the defendant through its council communicated to the plaintiff vide letter Ref. No. VI/RO/S.32 on 23rd October, 1989 as follows: I am directed to inform you that, after due consideration, the council has found you guilty of the said charges as communicated to you and indicated in the first paragraph above. The council after taking into account all the relevant facts and circumstances, as well as your plea for mitigation, has decided that you be removed forthwith from the office of the Dean of the Faculty and that you are barred from holding that or any other elective office or the office of the Head of Department, throughout your service tenure at the University of Ilorin. Is ultra vires, the powers of the defendant and the said decision made in error illegal, arbitrary, unconstitutional or null and void?

ii. A sum of two million (N2,000,000) naira only as general damages for wrongful and unjustifiable trial of the plaintiff by the defendant which has no standing and or competence to do so.

iii. A perpetual injunction restraining the defendant and its agents or servants from ever using paragraph 570 of council minutes of 19th October, 1989 as basis for trying plaintiff for the offence of plagiarism.

During the pendency of the trial, the Decree No. 107 of 1993 was promulgated to take effect from 17th November, 1993. Despite the enactment of this Decree, which affected the jurisdiction of State High Courts to hear and determine actions filed against agencies and parastatals of the Federal Government, the trial of the matter before the Kwara State High Court continued unabated until judgment was delivered by the trial judge on the 8th of May, 1996. Neither the parties nor the trial court adverted to the changes brought about by Decree No. 107 with regard to the jurisdiction of the trial court to hear and determine this action. At the end of the hearing, the learned trial judge following the addresses of learned counsel delivered a considered judgment wherein the claims of the plaintiff were upheld. As the respondent to this appeal was dissatisfied with the judgment of the trial court, it appealed to the Court of Appeal sitting at Kaduna. The appellant in couching its grounds of appeal touched upon and or raised the question as to the jurisdiction of the trial court to hear and determine the action before it.

However, when the appeal was set up for hearing, briefs having been filed and exchanged, the Court of Appeal then ordered as follows:

> There is an issue that needs to be considered. It is an issue of jurisdiction which needs to be addressed by both counsels. The parties should go and consider the provisions of Decree No. 107 of 1993 as well as the provisions of the Federal High Court Act. We need to be addressed on this important issue.

Thus, the counsel to the parties addressed the court. Thereafter, the Court of Appeal reviewed the relevant cases and the provisions of Decree No. 107 of 1993, Decree No. 60 of 1991 and Decree No. 16 of 1992, in conjunction with the provisions of the Federal High Court Act, and concluded that the proceedings and judgment delivered by the learned trial judge in respect of the action must be struck out as the trial court lacked jurisdiction to hear and determine the action. It is against this judgment that the appellant has filed this appeal to the Supreme Court.

ISSUE FOR DETERMINATION

Whether the lower courts lacked jurisdiction as a result of the promulgation of Decree No. 107 of 1993 on 17th

November, 1993 when the cause of action had arisen in 1989 and action on it filed before the trial court on 13th January, 1993?

HELD

1. **On the Jurisdiction of the Federal High Court over any Matters Concerning the Federal Government and/or any of Its Agencies.**

   It is therefore manifest that by reason of the above quoted provisions of section 230(1) of Decree No. 107 (now section 251(1) of the 1999 Constitution) the jurisdiction of the Federal High Court to hear and determine cases and matters had been enlarged. Hitherto, the jurisdiction of the Federal High Court was limited to that which was given to its predecessor. The Federal Revenue Court Act, Cap 134 of the Laws of Nigeria when that court was instituted, and kept intact by the provisions of S. 230(1) of the 1979 Constitution. But by reason of the new provision of section 230(1) subsection (q), (r), (s) of Decree No. 107, (now section 251(1)(q), (r),(s) of the 1999 Constitution)the jurisdiction of the court was increased to vest in the Federal High Court cases and matters concerning the Federal Government and or any of its agencies", per **Ejiwunmi, JSC** at page 452 para. C–E.

2. **On the Lack of Jurisdiction by the State High Court to Adjudicate on Declaration Actions against the Federal Goverment or Its Agencies**

It is manifest from the provisions of S. 230(1) of Decree No. 107 of 1993 , (now section 251(1) of the 1999 Constitution) and which I have already set out in this judgment, that the Federal High Court became vested with jurisdiction to hear and determine cases and matters including actions declaratory reliefs against the Federal Government and its agencies, thereby removing the trial of such actions by State High Courts, which, of course, included the High Court of Kwara State from the 17th of November, 1993.

In this respect, I need to refer to the case of *Madukolu v. Nkemdilim* (1962) 2 SCNLR 341, to which I had referred to earlier in this judgment when discussing the principles that should guide a court in its determination of whether a court was vested with the jurisdiction to determine a case or matter before it. One of the principles that is very apposite to the instant case is, whether there are any features in the case which affect the competence of the court. In the case in hand, it is not in doubt that Decree No. 107 of 1993 had removed the jurisdiction of State High Courts to hear and determine cases and matters including declaratory actions against the Federal Government or its agencies. It is also common ground that the respondent in the appeal, defendant in the trial court, is an agent of the Federal Government. It is therefore not arguable that the court below seised of an appeal of this with those features and viewed from the background of the law cannot help but hold that the trial court was not vested with the jurisdiction to try and determine the cause presented to it by the appellant," per. **Ejiwunmi, JSC,** at page 453 para. G–454 para. D.

Chapter 7

PART 3B

CRIMINAL CASES AND MATTERS RELATED TO SECTION 251(1) OF THE 1999 CONSTITUTION

By virtue of section 251(3) of the Constitution of the Federal Republic of Nigeria 1999, all criminal matters dealing with the items duly enumerated under section 251(1) of the said Constitution must be tried at the Federal High Court. Thus, where an accused person is alleged to have stolen from the revenue of the Federal Government, the appropriate court is the Federal High court, not a State High Court. It is of note that where a statue in addition to the provisions of the Constitution, specifies the appropriate court with powers to try an offence, the arraignment of an alleged offender before another court is liable to be vitiated for want of jurisdiction.

In the Court of Appeal of Nigeria

Lagos Judicial Division

ROTIMI WILMAT OLUBEKO v. FEDERAL REPUBLIC OF NIGERIA

Citation: (2014) LPELR-22632(CA)

Date: On Thursday, the 6th day of March, 2014

FACTS

The appellant, Rotimi Wilmat Olubeko, was arraigned in the Lagos Division of the Federal High Court on the 30th June, 2010, on a three count charge which reads as follows:

In the Federal High Court of Nigeria

In the Lagos Judicial Division

Holden at Lagos

Charge No. FHC/L/57C/2010

FEDERAL REPUBLIC OF NIGERIA

v.

ROTIMI WILMAT OLUBEKO 'M' 43 YRS.

Count One

That you, Rotimi Wilmat Olubeko 'm' and others still at large, sometimes in December, 2001 at Lagos, within the jurisdiction of the Federal High Court did conspire among yourselves to commit felony to wit: stealing and thereby committed an offence contrary to S. 516 A of the Criminal Code, Cap C38, Vol. 4 Laws of the Federation of Nigeria, 2004.

Count Two

That you, Rotimi Wilmat Olubeko 'm' and others still at large, at the same place and time and in the aforesaid Judicial Division did steal a copy of Certificate of Occupancy No. 63/63/1989 plot 19 block 42 Lekki Peninsula valued at two hundred million naira, property of Mrs. Francisca Adeoti Awolaja (deceased) and thereby committed an offence contrary to S. 390(9) of the Criminal Code, Cap C38, Vol. 4, Laws of the Federation of Nigeria, 2004.

Count Three

That you, Rotimi Wilmat Olubeko 'm', at the same place and time and in the aforesaid Judicial Division did obtain a building approval in respect of the property as aforesaid in the name of Francisca Adeoti Awolaja (deceased) by fraudulently representing yourself as Mrs. Francisca Adeoti Awolaja and thereby committed an offence contrary to S. 425 of the Criminal Code, Cap C38, Vol. 4 Laws of the Federation of Nigeria, 2004.

Dated 15th day of February, 2010

Signed: A.C. Onwuka Esq. (PROSECUTOR)
Legal Section, Force CID Annex
Alagbon Close, Ikoyi, Lagos
GSM: 07055322654

On the said 30th June, 2010, the appellant took his plea wherein he pleaded not guilty to all the three counts in the charge sheet.

Subsequently, by a notice of preliminary objection dated and filed on 20/9/2010, the appellant challenged the jurisdiction of the Federal High Court to entertain the matter. The Federal High court held that it had jurisdiction to hear the case, hence this appeal.

ISSUE FOR DETERMINATION

Whether the learned trial judge was right in law when he held that the Federal High Court has jurisdiction to entertain a criminal charge alleging offences committed in respect of a certificate of occupancy and building approval issued by the government of Lagos State.

HELD

On Exclusive Jurisdiction of the Federal High Court over Items (a) to (r) of Section 251(1) of the Constitution of the Federal Republic of Nigeria 1999 (as amended).

1. "Section 251(3) also specifically provides that:

> The Federal High Court shall also have and exercise jurisdiction and powers in respect of criminal cases and matters in respect of which jurisdiction is conferred by section 1 of this section.

Equally, in defining the powers of the Federal High Court for the purpose of exercising its jurisdiction as conferred in section 251, it is provided in section 252(1) as follows:

> 252(1) For the purpose of exercising any jurisdiction conferred upon it by this Constitution or as may be conferred by an act of the National Assembly, the Federal High Court shall have all the powers of the High Court of a state.

From my humble understanding of the provision of section 251(3) read in conjunction with section 251(1)(a) to (r), the Federal High Court have jurisdiction to entertain criminal matters in so far as they relate, connect or emanate from all the matters in which exclusive civil jurisdiction has been conferred on it under section 251(1)(a)-(r).

In other words and simply put, the Federal High Court does not only have exclusive civil jurisdiction over items (a) to (r) of section 251(1) of the Constitution of the Federal Republic of Nigeria 1999 (as amended) but also has criminal jurisdiction with respect thereto. In which case any offence committed in connection with the aforesaid items shall upon arraignment be tried by the Federal High Court", per **Oseji, JCA.**

On the Jurisdiction of the Federal High Court over Criminal Matters

2. "In the instant case, the provisions of section 251(3) of the 1999 Constitution is very clear and unambiguous to the effect that the criminal jurisdiction of the Federal High Court shall be with respect to those matter in which it has civil jurisdiction conferred on it in section 251(1)(a)-(r)

or as may be given by an Act of the National Assembly", per **Oseji, JCA.**

On the Jurisdiction of the Federal High Court over Criminal Matters not Involving Items Listed in S. 251(1) of the Constitution.

3. "Although land, being immovable, cannot be stolen, a document of title over a piece of land is collaterally linked to land and cannot be any of the issues connected with the civil jurisdiction of the Federal High Court under section 251(1) of the 1999 Constitution, as altered, as to confer criminal jurisdiction on the Federal High Court to determine an allegation of stealing of the document of title in question vide 251(3) of the 1999 Constitution. See also *Bukar Mandara v. Attorney General of the Federation* (1984) 1 SCNLR 311 where the Supreme Court held inter alia that aside from the jurisdiction conferred on the Federal High Court by the National Assembly, its criminal jurisdiction under the Constitution must be within the compass of the matters arising out of or connected with any of the matters to which civil jurisdiction is conferred on it by section 251(1) of the 1999 Constitution," per **Ikyegh, JCA.**

IN THE COURT OF APPEAL OF NIGERIA
Abuja Judicial Division

CA/A/551/2012

EHINDERO v. F.R.N.

Citation: (2014) 10 NWLR (Pt. 1415) Page 281

Date: On Friday the 14th Of February, 2014

FACTS

The Independent Corrupt Practices and other Related Offences Commission ICPC initiated a criminal prosecution against the appellant, a former Inspector General of Police and the 2nd respondent, who was the commissioner of police in charge of budget. The charge against the accused persons was for allegedly placing the sum of N557,995.00, donated to the Nigeria Police Force by the Government of Bayelsa State, into fixed deposit accounts at Wema Bank Plc and Intercontinental Bank Plc, the interest accruing from which transactions, were said to have been converted by the accused persons, and thereby corruptly conferred the benefit of the transaction on themselves. The accused persons were arraigned under the Corrupt Practices and Other related Offences Act 2000. The charge was initiated before the High Court of the Federal Capital territory.

The appellant filed a preliminary objection on the ground that the trial court lacked jurisdiction to try him in view of the provisions of section 251(1) (a) of the 1999

Constitution, which vested exclusive jurisdiction on the Federal High Court in civil cases or matters relating to the revenue of the Government of the Federation in which the said Government or any organ thereof or a person suing or being sued on behalf of the said Government is a party; in conjunction with the provision of section 251 (3) of the Constitution, which provides that the Federal High Court shall also have and exercise jurisdiction and powers in respect of criminal cases and matters in respect of which jurisdiction is conferred by subsection (1) of this section. The High Court refused the application to strike out and or dismiss the charge as sought by the preliminary objection, hence the appeal to the Court of Appeal.

ISSUE FOR DETERMINATION

Whether the trial court has jurisdiction to try the appellant under the charge in view of the express provisions of section 251(1)(a) & (3) of the 1999 Constitution?

HELD

"There is no provision in section 251 of the Constitution of the Federal Republic of Nigeria, 1999 which grants 'exclusive' jurisdiction to the Federal High Court in criminal cases or matters. Section 251(3) of the Constitution heavily relied upon by the appellant does not confer exclusive jurisdiction on the Federal High Court. For the avoidance of doubt, subsection (3) of section 251 of the Constitution provides thus:

> The Federal High Court shall also have and exercise jurisdiction and powers in respect of criminal cases and matters in respect of which jurisdiction is conferred by subsection (1) of this section.

As can be seen from the above provision, the phrase, 'to the exclusion of any other court' is completely omitted by the legislature and we cannot read into the subsection what is not there in, contained. If the legislature had intended by section 251(3) of the Constitution to confer 'exclusive' jurisdiction on the Federal High Court in criminal cases and matters, it would have clearly stated so. The provision of section 251(3) of the Constitution of the Federal republic of Nigeria, 1999 is very clear, plain and unambiguous and effect must be given to the ordinary meaning of the constitutional provision," per **Adumein , JCA** at pp. 304 para. C-H.

Author's note

Ehindero v. F.R.N was decided by the Abuja Division of the Court of Appeal on the 14th of February, 2014. The interpretation of section 251(3) of the 1999 Constitution according to the Court of Appeal in the above case appears logical, to the extent that the FCT High Court was held therein to have concurrent jurisdiction with the Federal High Court, considering the absence of the phrase 'exclusive' in the said provision.

It is, however, strongly noted that the decision of the Lagos Division of the Court of Appeal in *Olubeko v. F.R.N* (supra) reported above, which was decided on the 6th day of March, 2014, particularly per **Oseji JCA** is clear that the Federal High Court is vested with exclusive jurisdiction in respect of items listed in section 251(1) of the 1999 Constitution as amended.

The decision in *Olubeko v. F.R.N* conforms to four earlier decisions of the Supreme Court decided on 13th December, 2013, on the same issue.

The four relevant and earlier Supreme Court decisions, which considered the jurisdiction of the Lagos State High Court in respect of criminal cases and matters, under section 251(1) of the 1999 Constitution were not considered by the Court of Appeal in arriving at the decision in *Ehindero v. F.R.N* (supra).

The Supreme Court authorities which laid the interpretation of section 251(3) to rest, were all decided on 13th December, 2013. They are as follows:

I. Olabode George v. F.R.N;
II. Abidoye v. F.R.N;
III. Maideribe v. F.R.N;
IV. Aliyu v. F.R.N.

In the Supreme Court of Nigeria

Holden at Abuja

Suit No: SC. 180/2012

CHIEF OLABODE GEORGE v. FEDERAL REPUBLIC OF NIGERIA

Citation: (2014) 5 NWLR (Pt. 1399) Page 1

Date: On Friday, the 13th day of December, 2013

FACTS

The appellant was, at all material times, the Chairman of the Board of Directors of Nigerian Ports Authority ('the Authority' for short). He was charged before the trial court along with the Managing Director of the Authority and four available members of the Board as well as others said to be at large. They all held office from 2001-2003. On 8th August, 2008, the appellant along with five others and those said to be at large were arraigned on 163 count information. The appellant pleaded not guilty to all the counts. The Attorney General of the Federation amended the information dated 24th October, 2008, in which the counts were pruned down to 68. The appellant again, pleaded not guilty to the new counts.

In sum total, the appellant along with others were alleged to have exceeded the limit set to their authority to award contracts and contrived to bring the contracts within their limits by splitting them while also inflating their prices. The conviction and sentence of the appellant by the High Court of Lagos State, Ikeja Division ('the trial court' for short) on 26th October, 2009 was affirmed by the Court of Appeal.

ISSUE FOR DETERMINATION

Whether the High Court of Lagos State had the requisite jurisdiction to try the appellant long with others for the offences for which they were convicted.

HELD

On Jurisdiction of the Federal High Court over Criminal Cases and Matters relating to Control and Management of a Federal Government Agency

"The counts of splitting contract if in fact any contract was split relate to the control and management of a Federal Government agency, the Nigerian Ports Authority over which the Federal High Court has exclusive jurisdiction. See section 251 of the 1999 Constitution (supra) (as amended).

The Lagos State High Court had no jurisdiction to try the appellant and his trial, conviction and sentence must be declared null and void and I so declare", per **Ngwuta JSC** at pp. 28, para. G-H.

In the Supreme Court of Nigeria

Holden at Abuja

Suit No: SC. 182/2012

CAPTAIN O. ABIDOYE v. THE FEDERAL REPUBLIC OF NIGERIA

Citation: (2014) 5 NWLR (Pt. 1399) page 30

Date: On Friday, the 13th Day of December, 2013

FACTS

The appellant and five others and others said to be at large were arraigned on information containing 163 counts before the Ikeja Division of the High Court of Lagos State on 8th August, 2008. First and second accused persons before the trial court were the Chairman, Board of Directors of Nigerian Ports Authority and Managing Director of the Nigerian Ports Authority, respectively. Appellant as 3rd accused, and 4th, 5th and 6th accused persons (now appellants) were members of the Board of Directors of Nigerian Ports Authority. Each pleaded not guilty to each of the 163 counts of the information.

On 24th October, 2008, the information was amended by withdrawal of some of the counts therein contained. The amended information had 68 counts and each of the accused persons (now appellants) including the appellant herein pleaded not guilty to each count of the amended information.

For ease of reference, the 68 counts of the amended information can be split into the following four groups:

1. Offences contrary to section 22(3) of the Corrupt Practices and Other Related Offences Act, 2000: Counts 1-7.

2. Conspiracy to disobey lawful order issued by constituted authority contrary to section 517 of the Criminal Code Cap 32 Vol. 2, Laws of Lagos State of Nigeria 1994: Count 8.

3. Disobedience of lawful order issue by constituted authority contrary to section 203 of the Criminal Code Cap 32 Vol. 2, Laws of Lagos State of Nigeria 1994: Counts 9-57.

4. Abuse of office contrary to section 104 of the Criminal Code Cap. 32 Vol. 2, Laws of Lagos State of Nigeria 1994: Counts 58-68.

The Lagos State High Court convicted the accused persons. An appeal against the judgment was dismissed. Hence, the appellant appealed to the Supreme Court.

ISSUE FOR DETERMINATION

Whether the High Court of Lagos State had the requisite jurisdiction to try the appellants for the offences for which they were convicted?

HELD

On Jurisdiction of the Federal High Court over Criminal Cases and Matters relating to Control and Management of a Federal Government Agency

"Appellant was charged, tried, convicted and sentenced in his status as public officer. The relevant counts of the information laid against the appellant contained the averment that he committed the offences "while being an employee in the Public Service of the Federation of Nigeria as Board Member of Nigerian Ports Authority (NPA)." Appellant was not employed, at the material time, in the Public Service of Lagos State.

The offence of "abuse of office regarding award of contracts by splitting contracts" is an offence in relation to "the administration or the management and control of the Federal Government or any of its agencies" within the meaning and intendment of S.251(1)(p) of the Constitution of the Federal Republic of Nigeria 1999 (as amended). It is a matter over which the Federal High Court is conferred with jurisdiction to the exclusion of any State High Court, including the Lagos State High Court.

It follows that the proceedings leading to and including the conviction and sentence passed on the appellant were conducted without jurisdiction and therefore a nullity. See *Madukolu v. Nkemdilim* (1962) 1 All NLR 516; *National Bank v. Soyoye* (1977) 5 SC 181; *Penok Ltd v. Hotel Presidential Ltd* (1982) 12 SC 1", per **Ngwuta JSC** pp. at 63-64, para. E-A.

IN THE SUPREME COURT OF NIGERIA

HOLDEN AT ABUJA

Suit No: SC. 176/2013

ALHAJI ZANNA MAIDERIBE v. FEDERAL REPUBLIC OF NIGERIA

Citation: (2014) 5 NWLR (Pt.1399) Page 68

Date: On Friday, the 13th day of December, 2013

FACTS

The appellant was a member of the Board of the Nigerian Ports Authority, Lagos, one of the parastatals under the supervision of the Federal Ministry of Transport. The Authority was established by an Act of the National Assembly, the Nigerian Ports Authority Act, Chapter N.126, Laws of the Federation of Nigeria 2004. The Board of the Authority under which the appellant served, discharged its functions under the Act between 2001 when the Chairman and members of the Board were appointed and 2003 when the tenure of the Chairman and members of the Board terminated following the dissolution of the Board. At the end of the tenure of the appellant, the Chairman and other members of the Nigerian Ports Authority Board who served with the appellant between 2001 and 2003, a Contract Review Committee was appointed to examine the contracts awarded by the Board on which the appellant served, with the view of determining whether or not there had been any impropriety in the discharge of the responsibilities of the appellant, the chairman and other members while serving on the Board during the period of their tenure. Following the indictment of the appellant, Chairman and members of the Board in the report of the Contract Review Committee, the appellant, Chairman and other members were arraigned before the High Court of Justice of Lagos State at Ikeja where they were jointly charged in 68 counts in the amended information dated 28th October, 2008.

In counts 1-7, the appellant and his co-accused persons were charged with the offences of inflation of contracts. In count 8, on the other hand, the accused persons were charged under section 517 of the Criminal Code Law of Lagos State 1994 for conspiracy to commit the offences. They were also charged under Sections 104 and 203 of the Criminal Code of Lagos State for abuse of office and disobedience of lawful order issued by constituted authority. In counts 9-57, on the other hand, the accused persons were charged with the offences of disobedience to lawful order issued by constituted authority under section 203 of the Criminal Code Law of Lagos State 1994. The last charge against the accused persons in counts 59-68, is for the offences of abuse of office under section 104 of the Criminal Code Law of Lagos State 1994.

The learned trial judge in the judgment delivered on 26th October, 2009, discharged and acquitted the appellant and his co-accused persons of the offences of inflation of contracts among others in counts 1 to 7, 13,

14, 17, 18, 30, 31, 45, 47, 48, 58, 62,63, 66 and 68 of the amended information but found the appellant and his co-accused persons guilty as charged in respect of all the remaining counts. The appellant as well as the other co-accused persons were sentenced to 2 years imprisonment without an option of fine. Dissatisfied with this conviction and sentence by the trial court, the appellant as well as the other persons convicted along with him, lodged appeals against the judgment on substantially similar grounds of appeal. The appellant's appeal together with the appeals of the other persons convicted with the appellant were heard and dismissed by the Court of Appeal, Lagos Division in its judgment delivered on 26th October, 2009 in which the conviction and sentence of the appellant and other persons convicted and sentenced along with him were affirmed. Dissatisfied with the decision of the Court of Appeal, the appellant filed a further and final appeal to the Supreme Court against the affirmation of his conviction and sentence by the Court of Appeal.

ISSUE FOR DETERMINATION

Whether or not the learned justices of the Court of Appeal were right by not holding that the jurisdiction to try the 5th appellant for the offences for which the 5th appellant was tried and convicted is exclusively vested in the Federal High Court by virtue of the provisions of sections 251 of the Constitution of the Federal Republic of Nigeria, 1999 as amended?

HELD

On the Jurisdiction of the Federal High Court over Offences Relating to Agencies of the Federal Government

"The alleged abuse of office is with reference to a Federal Government Agency, that is, the Nigerian Ports Authority. The Federal High Court has jurisdiction to the exclusion of other courts in matters concerning the Authority", per **Sylvester Ngwuta, JSC.**

In the Supreme Court of Nigeria

Holden at Abuja

2013 Suit No: SC. 185/2012

ENGINEER SULE ALIYU v. FEDERAL REPUBLIC OF NIGERIA

Citation: (2014)NWLR 5 NWLR (Pt. 1399) Page 101

Date: On Friday, the 13th day of December

FACTS

The appellant herein, Engineer Sule Aliyu, now before the Court of Appeal was appointed a member of the Board of Directors of Nigerian Ports Authority. The Board on which the appellant served was in office from 2001-2003.

In the authority, there were guidelines in use until, the 12th day of November 2002 when Alhaji W. M. Kurawa, Pw4, who was the representative of the Ministry of Transport on the Board announced the existence of Exhibit P3, the new guideline for the award of contracts by the authority. Exhibit P3, was only made known to the Chairman and members of the Board after all the contracts listed for award had been awarded. The Board insisted that the contracts already awarded in terms of the previous guidelines were valid, not withstanding Exhibit P3, particularly as the new guidelines contained questionable features and had not been confirmed. The appellants and his co-accused were alleged to have contravened the new guidelines.

The appellant was arraigned before the High Court of Justice, Lagos State on the 8th of August, 2008 on 163 count information. The charges were all read and explained to each and everyone of the accused persons. All of them pleaded not guilty. Later, the prosecution reduced the charges and came up with 68 counts on 24/10/2008. Again, the appellant and other accused persons pleaded not guilty to the 68 count charge.

The alleged offences against the appellant and others in the trial court are mainly conspiracy.

ISSUES

Whether the High Court of Lagos State had the requisite jurisdiction to try the appellant for the offences for which they were convicted?

HELD

"The appellant, Engineer Sule Aliyu, has no business appearing before the Lagos State High Court. That court simply lacked jurisdiction to try the appellant. That court should have declined jurisdiction. The trial and conviction/sentences are therefore null and void. The decisions of the lower court's judgment cannot be saved", per **Muntaka-Coomassie, JSC** at pp. 117, para. F–G.

GLOSSARY

Ab initio
Abuse of office
Accessory claim
Act of the national assembly
Action
Adjudicatory process
Administrative actions
Administration
Admiralty
Affidavit
Agencies
Agency
Aggravated
Aircraft
Akitan JSC
Alien
Ammunition
Ancillary
Anton pillar
Appeal
Application
Arms
Attorney General

www.ingramcontent.com/pod-product-compliance
Lightning Source LLC
LaVergne TN
LVHW010542160826
845677LV00013B/2972